Understanding Corruption in Oregon

by Joseph Gall

Order this book online at www.trafford.com
or email orders@trafford.com

Most Trafford titles are also available at major online book retailers.

Printed in Victoria, BC, Canada.

ISBN: 978-1-4269-2743-0 (sc)

*Our mission is to efficiently provide the world's finest, most comprehensive book publishing
service, enabling every author to experience success. To find out how to publish your book, your
way, and have it available worldwide, visit us online at www.trafford.com*

Trafford rev. 4/8/2010

www.trafford.com

North America & international
toll-free: 1 888 232 4444 (USA & Canada)
phone: 250 383 6864 ♦ fax: 812 355 4082

CPO USN (Ret.)

1951 - 1971

Yep – that's me, more than 40 yrs ago , more than ten years after enlistment when war was raging on the Korean Peninsula. Some of you may remember that during the induction we took an oath to support and defend against all enemies foreign and domestic. War is again raging – in Afghanistan, Iraq and here at home. This time we are fighting domestic treason and foreign invaders(terrorists). If we don't learn the lessons of the past we will surely go down in history as a country without the will to fight for our freedom. We should listen when persons of learning and of good moral character speak, such as General Pete Pace, while serving as Chairman of the Joint Chief of Staff said –paraphrasing , I didn't take an oath to defend the President, I took the oath to support and defend The CONSTITUTION OF THE UNITED STATES OF AMERICA.

PREFACE

The corruption in Oregon is so vast it boggles the mind to think that people can be so callous and greedy with a narrow purpose for power and money.

I am not a lawyer. I am merely a high school graduate. However, within these pages you will be presented with information that you must verify to satisfy your questions for the truth and accuracy.

Nonetheless, we must challenge the corruption to avoid an appearance of ignorance and apathy. Knowledge is one ingredient required for the survival of our constitutional government.

My first petition for redress of grievances should have resolved the issue of illegal taxation of personal property but that didn't happen. My ignorance of applicable law allowed government deception and misrepresentation to prevail. The issue was and still is the illegal taxation of personal property; specifically, mobile homes classified as personal property by HUD and Oregon Revised Statute.

Please – research and verify everything contained on the pages within this book.

The Bible assures us that the truth will set us free and the BILL OF RIGHTS gives a right to petition for redress of grievances but we must go forward with common sense to distinguish between right and wrong with the courage to pursue justice.

Proceed with conviction to counter the arrogance of the educated government employees who readily attempt to deny us our rights; but, recognize that not all educated government employees will haughtily assume an unwarranted position of high esteem.

There is at least one patriot who says : Question with Boldness, Hold to the Truth, Speak Without Fear.

Another patriot - President Reagan - gave us some good advice that we should always keep in mind when dealing with people :

TRUST BUT VERIFY

Contents

Chapter 1 - Understanding Corruption

Corruption, as generally understood, has many components : of dishonesty; lacking integrity; depravity; lacking morality; the use of deception, bribery, fraud, abuse of power, intimidation, force(extortion either real or perceived), forgery, theft, and others not noted.

Dereliction of duty is the root enabler of corruption and other criminal activity committed by a citizen or a public servant .

The general welfare of society requires willing obedience of and respect for fair and impartial laws governing the populace and government. Without laws - dictators and chaos prevails.

If civility is expected - violation of law must be prosecuted without delay respecting moral and legal obligation.

We must not sit on our hands and expect someone else to rescue us from the bonds of government tyranny.

Chapter 2   -   Oath of Office

This is the foundation for a Republican Form of Government as guaranteed by The CONSTITUTION OF THE UNITED STATES, Article IV, Section 4.; and the Constitution of Oregon, Article XV, Section 3.

Violation of the oath is treasonous action. If the action involves two or more persons the treason becomes an organized resistance to our established constitutional government punishable as insurrection in accordance with The BILL OF RIGHTS, Article XIV, Section 3. and applicable Federal and Oregon law.

The oath is generally taken with the left hand on a Bible with right hand palm facing the person administrating the oath; therefore, violations of the oath are also spiritual abominations.

Chapter 3 - beginning

Assessor, David Lawson, occupied an elected position. He retired with a comfortable PERS annuity.

My story begins with his tax assessment (<u>Appendices A</u>) upon my mobile home, an assessment that was calculated on an assessed value (AV) that was higher than the real market value(RMV). I asked myself – how can this be?

This defies common sense! The real market value was the price paid for the structure during the downside of the mobile home market but the statement shows the RMV much more. Something upside down here.

When the assessor was asked about this – by what authority can this be possible? His answer was something like – I' m the assessor.

There, on the counter was literature pointing us to Measure 50 as their authority to be used with reference to any appeals. This information was used to file an appeal with the Board of Property Tax Appeals (BOPTA) who agreed that the RMV should show the price paid; however, I argued that the AV should be lowered to reflect the market and that I had agreed to pay a bonus for location and quality of the home. BOPTA disagreed.

Further appeals were taken to the Tax Court – Magistrate Division and the Regular Division that I will talk about later.

I learned much later that **<u>my home is tax exempt</u>** – classified as personal property in Oregon law(ORS 308.875); however, the Legislature did impose a $6.special assessment in ORS 446.525. And I learned that the assessor and BOPTA are required to know this – otherwise, they are considered incompetent.

> **ORS 308.875 Manufactured structures classified as real or personal property; effect of classification on other transactions.** If the manufactured structure and the land upon which the manufactured structure is situated are owned by the same person, the assessor shall assess the manufactured structure as real property. ***If the***

manufactured structure is owned separately and apart from the land upon which it is located, the assessor shall assess and tax the manufactured structure as personal property. A change in the property classification of a manufactured structure for ad valorem tax purposes does not change the property classification of the structure with respect to any transactions between the owner and security interest holders or other persons. *Manufactured structures classified as personal property need not be returned under ORS 308.290*. [1969 c.605 §16; 1971 c.529 §12; 1973 c.91 §6; 1983 c.748 §4; 1985 c.16 §456; 1993 c.696 §13; 2003 c.655 §67]

Note: See note under 308.865.

ORS 446.525 Special assessment; collection. (1) *A special assessment* is levied annually upon each manufactured dwelling that *is assessed for ad valorem property tax purposes as personal property*. The amount of the assessment is $6.

(2) On or before July 15 of each year, the county assessor shall determine and list the manufactured dwellings in the county that are assessed for the current assessment year as personal property. Upon making a determination and list, the county assessor shall cause the special assessment levied under subsection (1) of this section to be entered on the general assessment and tax roll prepared for the current assessment year as a charge against each manufactured dwelling so listed. Upon entry, the special assessment shall become a lien, be assessed and be collected in the same manner and with the same interest, penalty and cost charges as apply to ad valorem property taxes in this state.

(3) Any amounts of special assessment collected pursuant to subsection (2) of this section shall be deposited in the county treasury, shall be paid over by the county treasurer to the State Treasury and shall be credited to the Mobile Home Parks Account to be used exclusively for carrying out ORS 446.380, 446.385, 446.392 and 446.543 and implementing the policies described in ORS 446.515.

(4) In lieu of the procedures under subsection (2) of this section, the Director of the Housing and Community Services Department may make a direct billing of the special assessment to the owners of manufactured dwellings and receive

payment of the special assessment from those owners. In the event that under the billing procedures any owner fails to make payment, the unpaid special assessment shall become a lien against the manufactured dwelling and may be collected under contract or other agreement by a collection agency or may be collected under ORS 293.250, or the lien may be foreclosed by suit as provided under ORS chapter 88 or as provided under ORS 87.272 to 87.306. Upon collection under this subsection, the amounts of special assessment shall be deposited in the State Treasury and shall be credited to the Mobile Home Parks Account to be used exclusively for carrying out ORS 446.380, 446.385, 446.392 and 446.543 and implementing the policies described in ORS 446.515. [1989 c.918 §3; 1999 c.676 §28; 2007 c.71 §134; 2007 c.906 §43]

Note: See note under 446.515.

Chapter 4 - County government

The Yamhill County Organizational Chart (<u>Appendices B</u>) shows the Commissioners at the top with all other offices as peripheral and subordinate. So – common sense dictated appealing to them for some intervention.

The Commissioners – Kathy George, Leslie Lewis, Mary Stern – did nothing to enforce the law.

Perhaps their legal counselor John M. Gray, JR told them to ignore me; however, <u>he had a legal obligation</u> to report the criminal conduct to the District Attorney (DA), Bradley C. Berry who should have asked Sheriff Jack Crabtree to arrest the assessor, David Lawson, on Class B Felony violations of theft and extortion.

Wishful thinking? No, this is the way it should have happened but it didn't.

The Commissioners, District Attorney and Sheriff are elected officers. Yamhill County residents should remember these names when stepping into the voting booth. All were aware; therefore, they should be removed from office in the interest of justice – to return to a constitutional government.

Also, you should remember the well publicized case of the DA's prosecution of a couple of youngsters butt slapping the girls in the school hallways. The case was later dropped but it did highlight the misguided thought process of the DA , Sheriff and Commissioners.

Furthermore, I did make direct appeals to the Sheriff and the District Attorney who redirected my appeal to the Washington County District Attorney Jim Fun who denied criminal conduct existed.

Incompetency and malfeasance of a public officer may (must) be prosecuted as criminal conduct.

Chapter 5 - Accountability

Before moving on to other government offices we must examine and understand some laws of accountability. Herein are just a few.

First, but not necessarily the most important, is the law that implicitly says – know your job and perform your duties according to your job description. If you don't – you may be prosecuted and receive as punishment a year in jail and fined $6,250.00. Without doubt every public servant occupies a position of employment for personal gain. ALWAYS ! Meaning dollars for time. Can you imagine anyone working without receiving some <u>benefit</u>? However every action is not necessarily done to "harm another".

ORS 162.415 (1) (a) is nonfeasance – criminal conduct

ORS 162.415 (1) (b) is malfeasance – criminal conduct

ORS 162.415 Official misconduct in the first degree. (1) ***A public servant*** commits the crime of official misconduct in the first degree ***if with intent to obtain a benefit or to harm another:***

(a) The public servant knowingly fails to perform a duty imposed upon the public servant by law or one clearly inherent in the nature of office; or

(b) The public servant knowingly performs an act constituting an unauthorized exercise in official duties.

(2) Official misconduct in the first degree is a **Class A misdemeanor**. [1971 c.743 §215]

Second, a person who participates (whether or not ordered) in production of or changing anything that may be used to prosecute someone may be prosecuted, punished, and fined.

> **ORS 162.295 Tampering with physical evidence.** (1) _**A person**_ commits the crime of tampering with physical evidence if, with intent that it be used, introduced, rejected or unavailable in an official proceeding which is then pending or to the knowledge of such person is about to be instituted, the person:
>
> (a) Destroys, mutilates, alters, conceals or removes physical evidence impairing its verity or availability; or
>
> (b) Knowingly makes, produces or offers any false physical evidence; or
>
> (c) Prevents the production of physical evidence by an act of force, intimidation or deception against any person.
>
> (2) Tampering with physical evidence is a **Class A misdemeanor**. [1971 c.743 §204]

Third, this statute says basically the same as the preceding statute with one difference – public records. Example: 1) changing or interrupting a court trial recording; 2) adding a word or phrase to a statute for purpose of changing the meaning or intent, 3) deleting any portion of the tax record. Violations may be prosecuted and given one year in jail and a fine of $6,250.00. The assessors ignored this when they removed from the tax records an entry that should have been preserved to show that an appeal was made and honored by BOPTA .

> **ORS 162.305 Tampering with public records.** (1) _**A person**_ commits the crime of tampering with public records if, without lawful authority, the person knowingly destroys, mutilates, conceals, removes, makes a false entry in or falsely alters any public record, including records relating to the Oregon State Lottery.
>
> (2)(a) Except as provided in paragraph (b) of this subsection, tampering with public records is a **Class A misdemeanor**.

(b) Tampering with records relating to the Oregon State Lottery is a Class C felony. [1971 c.743 §205; 1991 c.962 §16]

Fourth, this obstruction statute is intended to preclude badgering from the judicial bench or some other government office. Please read this carefully because I'll return to it later. Again a Class A misdemeanor.

> **ORS 162.235 Obstructing governmental or judicial administration.**
> (1) ***A person*** commits the crime of obstructing governmental or judicial administration if the person intentionally obstructs, impairs or hinders the administration of law or other governmental or judicial function **by means of intimidation, force, physical or economic interference or obstacle.**
>
> (2) This section shall not apply to the obstruction of unlawful governmental or judicial action or interference with the making of an arrest.
>
> (3) Obstructing governmental or judicial administration is a **Class A misdemeanor**. [1971 c.743 §198; 1981 c.902 §1]

Fifth, note that this deals with public officers , e.g. judges, lawyers, department heads, and others who have taken an oath of office as prerequisite to hold office. Notice that this does not categorize a punishment to be imposed but does refer to applicable criminal law. Unfortunately prosecution is unlikely because we must rely on the Justice Department; also, unlikely because the word "may" is used instead of the word "shall".

Constitution of Oregon, Article VII (Amended), Section 6.

> **Section 6. Incompetency or malfeasance of public officer.** ***Public officers shall not be impeached***; but incompetency, corruption, malfeasance or delinquency in office ***may*** be tried in the same manner as criminal offenses, and judgment ***may*** be given of dismissal from office, and such further punishment as may have been prescribed by law. [Created through initiative petition filed July 7, 1910, and adopted by the people Nov. 8, 1910]

Chapter 6 - *Incompetency or malfeasance of public officer*

The Constitution of Oregon takes precedence over all Oregon Revised Statutes (ORS) and Oregon Administrative Rules (OAR).

Any law or rule that does not comply with The CONSTITUTION OF THE UNITED STATES or the Constitution of Oregon has no legal effect.

The general rule is that an unconstitutional statute, though having the form and name of law, is in reality no law, but is wholly void, and ineffective for any purpose; since unconstitutionality dates from the time of its enactment, and not merely from the date of the decision so branding it.

"No one is bound to obey an unconstitutional law and no courts are bound to enforce it."

16 Am Jur 2d, Sec 177

Late 2d, sec 256

We rely on the Justice Department to prosecute criminal conduct – a reliance unfounded in reality. What happens when the Justice Department refuses to prosecute reported criminal conduct by a public servant (officer)? The answer is - ***nothing as of this writing.***

The Justice Department and the District Attorney has walked through the escape hatch provided in the Constitution of Oregon, Article VII (Amended), Section 6.

that states "may be tried . . .". The word "may" is used to give permission rather than being mandatory.

Constitution of Oregon, Article VII (Amended), Section 6.

Section 6. Incompetency or malfeasance of public officer. _Public officers shall not be impeached_; but incompetency, corruption, malfeasance or delinquency in office _may_ be tried in the same manner as criminal offenses, and judgment _may_ be given of dismissal from office, and such further punishment as may have been prescribed by law. [Created through initiative petition filed July 7, 1910, and adopted by the people Nov. 8, 1910]

Nonetheless, the same Constitution of Oregon, Article V.

Section 10. Governor to see laws executed. He _shall_ take care that the Laws be faithfully executed.–

The Attorney General is the Governor's legal advisor. The Oregon Legislature has foolishly _– maybe intentional –_ given sole prosecutorial authority to the Executive Branch which includes the District Attorney.

Violations of the Code of Judicial Conduct or the Code of Professional Conduct are rarely made known to the general public and any prosecutions are even more protected. The Commission on Judicial Fitness and Disability and the Oregon State Bar (OSB) have ignored my reports of MISCONDUCT of judges and lawyers. These public officers operate with impunity – even today they hold office.

ORS 161.155 Criminal liability for conduct of another. _A person_ is criminally liable for the conduct of another person constituting a crime if:

(1) The person is made criminally liable by the statute defining the crime; or

(2) With the intent to promote or facilitate the commission of the crime **the person:**

(a) Solicits or commands such other person to commit the crime; or

(b_) Aids or abets or agrees or attempts to aid or abet such other person in planning or committing the crime; or_

(c) _Having a legal duty to prevent_ the commission of the crime, fails to make an effort the person is legally required to make. [1971 c.743 §13]

ORS 161.545 "Misdemeanor" described. A crime is a misdemeanor if it is so designated in any statute of this state or if a person convicted thereof may be sentenced to a maximum term of imprisonment of <u>not more than one year</u>. [1971 c.743 §69]

Chapter 7   -   Stipulate, stipulation, stipulated

These words raise a red flag for me so that I must carefully read the document. I've learned that these words mean that I agree with the content of the document.

Very early in this appeal process the assessors attempted to reach a stipulated agreement that would have precluded further challenge of the illegal taxation of my mobile home. The content of the documents were diametrical to the facts. The assessors and the judges were very annoyed that I refused to sign the documents as presented.

The document identified here for discussion is Appendices C. This raised a red flag, didn't pass the smell test, for many reasons. This was a document intended to be used by the assessors in any further appeals. Let's examine the document that says –

BEFORE THE YAMHILL COUNTY BOARD OF PROPERTY TAX APPEALS;

1. ***Real Property Stipulated Agreement;***
2. Petitioner's Name and Address
3. Petition No. 34.1
4. Account No. 508939 (note: this is on my tax statement)
5. Tax year 2002
6. The above-named petitioner and the assessor of Yamhill County have entered into the following agreement concerning the valuation of the above-described property.
7. Etc. etc

This document was generated by the assessor before I had a copy of Measure 50 that was referred to in the assessor's Sales Questionaire :see Appendices D.

Getting a copy of Measure 50 was easy at the local library, The librarian printed a copy for a fee with a smile and helpful attitude.

Now I knew that Measure 50 was a **real** property issue passed by the people to rein-in the upward rocketing tax assessments that threatened home ownership. When this passed I was not an Oregon resident.

Examining Measure 50 in Section 11. (1) (a) there is created a new term that assessors and judges *mis*-use – "maximum assessed value". This term now known as MAV identifies the RMV reduced by 10 percent ***beginning July 1, 1995***. A rational, objective person would say the intended use of MAV is to identify a starting point for calculating a subsequent allowed three percent increase of the ad valorem taxes – a ***starting point*** that is used only once and ***the figure never changes.***

Back to the proposed Stipulated Agreement***. My property was first entered on the tax rolls in 1998 a year after the first allowed three percent increase of the taxes***. But in this proposed agreement the term is used showing a figure of $55,036. There should be ***no MAV*** used in any way related to my ***personal property***.

Yes, we should consider the assessors "incompetency or malfeasance of public officer" and "misconduct in the first degree".

Of course I was unaware at that time that my property was classified as **personal** property. But my ignorance is no excuse for the assessors.

Back to the proposed Stipulated Agreement that says "The parties to this appeal agree to the correction of values as indicated above and request the board of property tax appeals issue an order reflecting this change".

Now you know how important it is to raise the red flag of suspicion when you see the words stipulate, stipulation or stipulated.

Go back and re-read Chapters 5 and 6 and then consider these –

164.085 Theft by deception. (1*) A person*, who obtains property of another thereby, commits theft by deception when, with intent to defraud, the person:

(a) Creates or confirms another's false impression of law, value, intention or other state of mind that the actor does not believe to be true;

(b) ***Fails to correct a false impression that the person previously created or confirmed;***

(c) Prevents another from acquiring information pertinent to the disposition of the property involved;

(d) Sells or otherwise transfers or encumbers property, failing to disclose a lien, adverse claim or other legal impediment to the enjoyment of the property, whether such impediment is or is not valid, or is or is not a matter of official record; or

(e) Promises performance that the person does not intend to perform or knows will not be performed.

(2*) "Deception" does not include* falsity as to matters <u>having no pecuniary significance</u>, or representations unlikely to deceive ordinary persons in the group addressed. For purposes of this subsection, the theft of a companion animal, as defined in ORS 164.055, or a captive wild animal is a matter having pecuniary significance.

(3) In a prosecution for theft by deception, the defendant's intention or belief that a promise would not be performed may not be established by or inferred from the fact alone that such promise was not performed.

(4) In a prosecution for theft by deception committed by means of a bad check, it is prima facie evidence of knowledge that the check or order would not be honored if:

(a) The drawer has no account with the drawee at the time the check or order is drawn or uttered; or

(b) Payment is refused by the drawee for lack of funds, upon presentation within 30 days after the date of utterance, and the drawer fails to make good within 10 days after receiving notice of refusal. [1971 c.743 §128; 1991 c.837 §10; 2007 c.71 §49]

As my appeals moved into the courts I did stipulate that my home was sited in Kathleen Manor a mobile home park. Mobile homes are now identified as manufactured structures in the statutes.

Deception is where the opposition has operated throughout the proceedings. Before we go there I will stipulate that the opposition is referred to as Defendant in the Tax Court but in the Supreme Court they are Respondent.

Back to theft by deception. The assessors rolled into the RMV the price of the detached ***carport*** which is identified as ***real property*** – mixing real property with personal property. Again, incompetently violating existing law. Ask yourself – who benefited by this?

Take a deep breath – let me digress a bit to share some ignorance. This old timer isn't the sharpest tack in town.

It has taken more than eight years to finally realize that the college educated government public officers snookered me. The fast shuffle of information they offered did misguide me to believe that my property was real property. WHY? Was it for money or power?

Without doubt it was both but primarily for the money to support their income and their lucrative PERS retirement. But, also the abuse of power to do as they pleased. They most probably never imagined that a yokel like me would challenge their criminal acts.

> Appendices A, the Tax Statement for 2002 to 2003 shows an RMV of
> $69,742 for the structure**s.**

> Appendices E, the dealer invoice for my home shows the cost as $43,533
>   a difference of $26,209 which tells me that the difference had to be
>   the cost of the carport.

Now consider this – in 2001 my purchase price for the home was $43,000 for the package (home and carport).

It's rational to say that the home RMV was $43,000 minus $26,209 equals $16,791.

It's also rational that I should have argued that the RMV for my home was actually $16,791 instead of the $33,500 shown on   Appendices F, the News-Register classified add.

We could easily attest that the actions of the public officers was dishonest, deceitful with misrepresentations.

Yes, money is personal property protected by The BILL OF RIGHTS, Article IV and Article X. The government has not provided a specific law that authorized the taxation of manufactured structures classified in law, Federal and State, as personal property; consequently the assessment and collection are theft by extortion.

> **ORS 164.075 Theft by extortion.** (1) ***A person*** commits theft by
>   extortion when the person compels or induces another to deliver
>   property to the person or to a third person by instilling in the other
>   a fear that, if the property is not so delivered, the actor or a third
>   person will in the future:

(a) Cause physical injury to some person;

(b) Cause damage to property;

(c) Engage in other conduct constituting a crime;

(d) Accuse some person of a crime or cause criminal charges to be instituted against the person;

(e) Expose a secret or publicize an asserted fact, whether true or false, tending to subject some person to hatred, contempt or ridicule;

(f) Cause or continue a strike, boycott or other collective action injurious to some person's business, except that such conduct is not considered extortion when the property is demanded or received for the benefit of the group in whose interest the actor purports to act;

(g) Testify or provide information or withhold testimony or information with respect to another's legal claim or defense;

(h) ***Use or abuse the position as a public servant by performing some act within or related to official duties, or by failing or refusing to perform an official duty, in such manner as to affect some person adversely; or***

(i) Inflict any other harm that would not benefit the actor.

(2) Theft by extortion is a **Class B felony**. [1971 c.743 §127; 1987 c.158 §27; 2007 c.71 §48]

Class B felony can be punished with ten years in jail and a fine of $250,000.00 for each count of the indictment which would be multiplied by the number of manufactured structures upon which a tax was **assessed illegally**. In Oregon there are more than 65,000 manufactured structures.

ORS 305.120 Enforcement of tax laws. (1) ***The Department of Revenue shall see*** that revenue officers comply with the tax and revenue laws, that all taxes are collected, that complaint is made against any person violating such laws and that penalties prescribed by such laws are enforced.

(2) The Director of the Department of Revenue may call upon the district attorney or Attorney General to institute and conduct prosecutions for violations of the laws in respect to the assessment and taxation of property and the collection of public taxes and revenues. [Formerly 306.140]

307.010 Definition of "real property" and "land"; timber and mineral interests in real property. (1) *As used in the property tax laws of this state:*

(a) "Land" means land in its natural state. For purposes of assessment of property subject to assessment at assessed value under ORS 308.146, land includes any site development made to the land. As used in this paragraph, "site development" includes fill, grading, leveling, underground utilities, underground utility connections and any other elements identified by rule of the Department of Revenue.

(b) "Real property" includes:

(A) The land itself, above or under water;

(B) All buildings, structures, improvements, machinery, equipment or fixtures erected upon, above or affixed to the land;

(C) All mines, minerals, quarries and trees in, under or upon the land;

(D) All water rights and water powers and all other rights and privileges in any way appertaining to the land; or

(E) Any estate, right, title or interest whatever in the land or real property, less than the fee simple.

(2) Where the grantor of land has, in the instrument of conveyance, reserved or conveyed:

(a) Any of the timber standing upon the land, with the right to enter upon the ground and remove the timber, the ownership of the standing timber so reserved or conveyed is an interest in real property.

(b) The right to enter upon and use any of the surface ground necessary for the purpose of exploring, prospecting for, developing or otherwise extracting any gold, silver, iron, copper, lead, coal, petroleum, gases, oils or any other metals, minerals or mineral deposits in or upon the land, such right is an interest in real property. [Amended by 1987 c.756 §19; 1991 c.459 §37; 1997 c.541 §98; 2003 c.46 §10]

ORS 307.020 Definition of "personal property"; inapplicability to certain utilities. (1) As used in the property tax laws of this state, ***unless otherwise specifically provided:***

(a) "Intangible personal property" or "intangibles" includes but is not limited to:

(A) Money at interest, bonds, notes, claims, demands and all other evidences of indebtedness, secured or unsecured, including notes, bonds or certificates secured by mortgages.

(B) All shares of stock in corporations, joint stock companies or associations.

(C) Media constituting business records, computer software, files, records of accounts, title records, surveys, designs, credit references, and data contained therein. "Media" includes, but is not limited to, paper, film, punch cards, magnetic tape and disk storage.

(D) Goodwill.

(E) Customer lists.

(F) Contracts and contract rights.

(G) Patents, trademarks and copyrights.

(H) Assembled labor force.

(I) Trade secrets.

(b) "Personal property" means "tangible personal property."

(c) "Tangible personal property" includes ***but is not limited to all chattels and movables,*** such as boats and vessels, merchandise and stock in trade, furniture and personal effects, goods, livestock, vehicles, farming implements, movable machinery, movable tools and movable equipment.

(2) Subsection (1) of this section does not apply to any person, company, corporation or association covered by ORS 308.505 to 308.665. [Amended by 1959 c.82 §1; 1977 c.602 §1; 1993 c.353 §1; 1997 c.154 §27; 2005 c.94 §30]

ORS 307.190 Tangible personal property held for personal use; inapplicability of exemption to property required to be registered, floating homes, boathouses and manufactured structures. (1) All items of tangible personal property held by the owner, or for delivery by a vendor to the owner, ***for personal use***, benefit or enjoyment, ***are exempt from taxation.***

(2) The exemption provided in subsection (1) of this section does <u>not apply to:</u>

(a) Any tangible personal property held by the owner, ***wholly or partially for use or sale*** in the ordinary course of a trade or business, for the production of income, or solely for investment.

(b) Any tangible personal property <u>required to be licensed or registered</u> under the laws of this state.

(c) Floating homes or boathouses, as defined in ORS 830.700.

(d) Manufactured structures as defined in ORS 446.561. [Amended by 1953 c.698 §7; 1969 c.648 §1; 1977 c.615 §2; 1985 c.614 §1; 1987 c.601 §5; 2003 c.655 §63]

ORS 308.232 Property to be valued at 100 percent real market value and assessed at assessed value. All real or personal property within each county **not exempt from ad valorem property taxation** or ***subject to special assessment*** shall be valued at 100 percent of its real market value. Unless the property is subject to maximum assessed value adjustment under ORS 308.149 to 308.166, the property shall be assessed at the property's assessed value determined under ORS 308.146. [1953 c.701 §2; 1959 c.519 §1; 1961 c.243 §1; 1967 c.293 §6; 1979 c.241 §33; 1981 c.804 §39; 1985 c.613 §8; 1991 c.459 §97; 1997 c.541 §159]

ORS 308.875 Manufactured structures classified as real or personal property; effect of classification on other transactions. If the manufactured structure and the land upon which the manufactured structure is situated are owned by the same person, the assessor shall assess the manufactured structure as real property. ***If the manufactured structure is owned separately and apart from the land upon which it is located, the assessor shall assess and tax the manufactured structure as personal property***. A change in the property classification of a manufactured structure for ad valorem tax purposes does not change the property classification of the structure with respect to any transactions between the owner and security interest holders or other persons. ***Manufactured structures classified as personal property need not be returned under ORS 308.290***. [1969 c.605 §16; 1971 c.529 §12; 1973 c.91 §6; 1983 c.748 §4; 1985 c.16 §456; 1993 c.696 §13; 2003 c.655 §67]

Note: See note under 308.865.

ORS 308.290 Returns; personal property; real property; combined real and personal returns for industrial property; contents; filing; extensions; confidentiality and disclosure; lessor-lessee elections; rules. (1)(a) Every person and the managing agent or officer of any business, firm, corporation or association owning, or having in possession or under control ***taxable personal property*** shall make a return of the property for ad valorem tax purposes to the assessor of the county in which the property has its situs for taxation. As between a mortgagor and mortgagee or a lessor and lessee, however, the actual owner and the person in possession may agree between them as to who shall make the return and pay the tax, and the election shall be followed by the person in possession of the roll who has notice of the election. Upon the failure of either party to file a personal property tax return on or before March 1 of any year, both parties shall be jointly and severally subject to the provisions of ORS 308.296.

(b) Every person and the managing agent or officer of any business, firm, corporation or association owning or in possession of taxable real property shall make a return of the property for ad valorem tax purposes when so requested by the assessor of the county in which the property is situated.

(2)(a) Each return of personal property shall contain a full listing of the property and a statement of its real market value, including a separate listing of those items claimed to be exempt as imports or exports. Each statement shall contain a listing of the additions or retirements made since the prior January 1, indicating the book cost and the date of acquisition or retirement. Each return shall contain the name, assumed business name, if any, and address of the owner of the personal property and, if it is a partnership, the name and address of each general partner or, if it is a corporation, the name and address of its registered agent.

(b) Each return of real property shall contain a full listing of the several items or parts of the property specified by the county assessor and a statement exhibiting their real market value. Each return shall contain a listing of the additions and retirements made during the year indicating the book cost, book value of the additions and retirements or the appraised real market value of retirements as specified in the return by the assessor.

(c) There shall be annexed to each return the affidavit or affirmation of the person making the return that the statements contained in the return are true. All returns shall be in a form that the county assessor, with the approval of the Department of Revenue, may prescribe. Prior to December 31 preceding the assessment year, the department or assessor shall cause blank forms for the returns to be prepared and distributed by mail, but failure to receive or secure the form does not relieve the person, managing agent or officer from the obligation of making any return required by this section.

(3) All returns shall be filed on or before March 1 of each year, but the county assessor or the Department of Revenue may grant an extension of time to April 15 within which to file the return as provided by subsection (5), (6) or (7) of this section.

(4)(a) In lieu of the returns required under subsection (1)(a) or (b) of this section, every person and the managing agent or officer of any business, firm, corporation or association owning or having in possession or under control taxable real and personal property that is either principal industrial property or secondary industrial property as defined by ORS 306.126 (1) and is appraised by the Department of Revenue shall file a combined return of the real and personal property with the department.

(b) The contents and form of the return shall be as prescribed by rule of the department. Any form shall comply with ORS 308.297. Notwithstanding ORS 308.875, a manufactured structure that is a part of an industrial property shall be included in a combined return.

(c) In order that the county assessor may comply with ORS 308.295, the department shall provide a list to the assessor of all combined returns that are required to be filed with the department under this subsection but that were not filed on or before the due date or within the time allowed by an extension.

(d) If the department has delegated appraisal of the property to the county assessor under ORS 306.126 (3), the department shall notify the person otherwise required to file the combined return under this subsection as soon as practicable after the delegation that the combined return is required to be filed with the assessor.

(e) Notwithstanding subsection (1) of this section, a combined return of real and personal property that is industrial property appraised by the department shall be filed with the department on or before March 1 of the year.

(5)(a) Any person required to file a return under subsection (4) of this section may apply to the Department of Revenue for an extension of time to April 15, within which to file the return.

(b) Extensions granted under this subsection may be based on a finding by the department that:

(A) Good or sufficient cause exists for granting an extension for the property tax year of the return; or

(B) Granting an extension enhances the accuracy of the filing by the taxpayer and long-term voluntary compliance. An extension granted under this subparagraph shall continue in effect for each subsequent property tax year until the taxpayer cancels the extension or the department revokes the extension.

(c) An extension granted under this subsection shall apply to returns required to be filed under subsection (4) of this section with either the county assessor or the department.

(d) The department shall notify assessors in affected counties when the department grants extensions under this subsection.

(6)(a) Except as provided in subsection (5) of this section, any person required to file a return with the county assessor under this section may apply to the assessor for an extension of time to April 15 within which to file the return.

(b) Extensions granted under this subsection may be based on a finding by the assessor that:

(A) Good or sufficient cause exists for granting an extension for the property tax year of the return; or

(B) Granting an extension enhances the accuracy of the filing by the taxpayer and long-term voluntary compliance. An extension granted under this subparagraph shall continue in effect for each subsequent property tax year until the taxpayer cancels the extension or the assessor revokes the extension.

(7)(a) Any person required to file returns in more than one county may apply to the Department of Revenue for an extension of time to April 15 within which to file the returns. The department may grant extensions to a person required to file returns in more than one county.

(b) Extensions granted under this subsection may be based on a finding by the department that:

(A) Good or sufficient cause exists for granting an extension for the property tax year of the return; or

(B) Granting an extension enhances the accuracy of the filing by the taxpayer and long-term voluntary compliance. An extension granted under this subparagraph shall continue in effect for each subsequent property tax year until the taxpayer cancels the extension or the department revokes the extension.

(c) Whenever the department grants an extension to a person required to file returns in more than one county, the department shall notify the assessors in the counties affected by the extensions.

(8) The Department of Revenue shall, by rule, establish procedures and criteria for granting, denying or revoking extensions under this section after consultation with an advisory committee selected by the department that represents the interests of county assessors and affected taxpayers.

(9) A return is not in any respect controlling on the county assessor or on the Department of Revenue in the assessment of any property. On any failure to file the required return, the property shall be listed and assessed from the best information obtainable from other sources.

(10)(a) All returns filed under the provisions of this section and ORS 308.525 and 308.810 are confidential records of the Department of Revenue or the county assessor's office in which the returns are filed or of the office to which the returns are forwarded under paragraph (b) of this subsection.

(b) The assessor or the department may forward any return received in error to the department or the county official responsible for appraising the property described in the return.

(c) Notwithstanding paragraph (a) of this subsection, a return described in paragraph (a) of this subsection may be disclosed to:

(A) The Department of Revenue or its representative;

(B) The representatives of the Secretary of State or to an accountant engaged by a county under ORS 297.405 to 297.555 for the purpose of auditing the county's personal property tax assessment roll (including adjustments to returns made by the Department of Revenue);

(C) The county assessor, the county tax collector, the assessor's representative or the tax collector's representative for the purpose of:

(i) Collecting delinquent real or personal property taxes; or

(ii) Correctly reflecting on the tax roll information reported on returns filed by a business operating in more than one county or transferring property between counties in this state during the tax year;

(D) Any reviewing authority to the extent the return being disclosed relates to an appeal brought by a taxpayer;

(E) The Division of Child Support of the Department of Justice or a district attorney to the extent the return being disclosed relates to a case for which the Division of Child Support or the district attorney is providing support enforcement services under ORS 25.080; or

(F) The Legislative Revenue Officer for the purpose of preparation of reports, estimates and analyses required by ORS 173.800 to 173.850.

(d) Notwithstanding paragraph (a) of this subsection:

(A) The Department of Revenue may exchange property tax information with the authorized agents of the federal government and the several states on a reciprocal basis, or with county assessors, county tax collectors or authorized representatives of assessors or tax collectors.

(B) Information regarding the valuation of leased property reported on a property return filed by a lessor under this section may be disclosed to the lessee or other person in possession of the property. Information regarding the valuation of leased property reported on a property return filed by a lessee under this section may be disclosed to the lessor of the property.

(11) If the assessed value of any personal property in possession of a lessee is less than the maximum amount of the assessed value of taxable personal property for which ad valorem property taxes may be canceled under ORS 308.250, the person in possession of the roll may disregard an election made under subsection (1) of this section and assess the owner or lessor of the property. [Amended by 1953 c.218 §2; 1961 c.683 §2; 1963 c.436 §1; 1965 c.16 §1; 1967 c.50 §1; 1971 c.568 §2; 1971 c.574 §2; 1975 c.789 §12; 1977 c.124 §6; 1977 c.774 §24; 1979 c.286 §14; 1981 c.623 §2; 1981 c.804 §49; 1987 c.312 §3; 1991 c.191 §5; 1991 c.459 §108; 1993 c.726 §56; 1993 c.813 §2; 1995 c.609 §3; 1997 c.154 §30; 1997 c.541 §169; 1997 c.819 §2; 2001 c.479 §2; 2003 c.541 §1; 2005 c.94 §47; 2007 c.226 §1; 2007 c.227 §1; 2007 c.613 §1a; 2007 c.824 §1]

Note: Section 2, chapter 226, Oregon Laws 2007, provides:

Sec. 2. The amendments to ORS 308.290 by section 1 of this 2007 Act apply to property tax returns filed on or after January 1, 2008. [2007 c.226 §2]

Note: Section 3, chapter 227, Oregon Laws 2007, provides:

> **Sec. 3.** The amendments to ORS 308.290 and 308.810 by sections 1 and 2 of this 2007 Act apply to property tax returns filed on or after January 1, 2008, for tax years beginning on or after July 1, 2008. [2007 c.227 §3]

Note: See note under 308.250

> **ORS 308.250 Valuation and assessment of personal property; cancellation of assessment and short form return in certain cases; verified statements.** (1) All personal property ***not exempt from ad valorem taxation or subject to special assessment*** shall be valued at 100 percent of its real market value, as of January 1, at 1:00 a.m. and shall be assessed at its assessed value determined as provided in ORS 308.146.

Note: Section 3, chapter 613, Oregon Laws 2007, provides:

> **Sec. 3.** The amendments to ORS 308.250 and 308.290 by sections 1a and 2 of this 2007 Act apply to returns filed for property tax years beginning on or after July 1, 2008. [2007 c.613 §3; 2007 c.613 §3a]

> **ORS 446.525 Special assessment; collection.** (1) ***A special assessment*** is levied annually upon each manufactured dwelling that is assessed for ad valorem property tax purposes as ***personal property***. The amount of the assessment is $6.

> (2) On or before July 15 of each year, the county assessor shall determine and list the manufactured dwellings in the county that are assessed for the current assessment year as personal property. Upon making a determination and list, the county assessor shall cause the special assessment levied under subsection (1) of this section to be entered on the general assessment and tax roll prepared for the current assessment year as a charge against each manufactured dwelling so listed. Upon entry, the special assessment shall become a lien, be assessed and be collected in the same manner and with the same interest, penalty and cost charges as apply to ad valorem property taxes in this state.

(3) Any amounts of special assessment collected pursuant to subsection (2) of this section shall be deposited in the county treasury, shall be paid over by the county treasurer to the State Treasury and shall be credited to the Mobile Home Parks Account to be used exclusively for carrying out ORS 446.380, 446.385, 446.392 and 446.543 and implementing the policies described in ORS 446.515.

(4) In lieu of the procedures under subsection (2) of this section, the Director of the Housing and Community Services Department may make a direct billing of the special assessment to the owners of manufactured dwellings and receive payment of the special assessment from those owners. In the event that under the billing procedures any owner fails to make payment, the unpaid special assessment shall become a lien against the manufactured dwelling and may be collected under contract or other agreement by a collection agency or may be collected under ORS 293.250, or the lien may be foreclosed by suit as provided under ORS chapter 88 or as provided under ORS 87.272 to 87.306. Upon collection under this subsection, the amounts of special assessment shall be deposited in the State Treasury and shall be credited to the Mobile Home Parks Account to be used exclusively for carrying out ORS 446.380, 446.385, 446.392 and 446.543 and implementing the policies described in ORS 446.515. [1989 c.918 §3; 1999 c.676 §28; 2007 c.71 §134; 2007 c.906 §43]

Note: See note under 446.515.

307.032 Maximum assessed value and assessed value of partially exempt property and specially assessed property. (1) _Unless determined under a provision of law_ governing the partial exemption that applies to the property, the maximum assessed value and assessed value of partially exempt property shall be determined as follows:

(a) The maximum assessed value:

(A) For the first tax year in which the property is partially exempt, shall equal the real market value of the property, reduced by the value of the partial exemption, multiplied by the ratio, not greater than 1.00, of the average maximum assessed value over the average real market value for the tax year of property in the same area and property class.

(B) For each tax year after the first tax year in which the property is subject to the same partial exemption, shall equal 103 percent of the property's assessed value for the prior year or 100 percent of the property's maximum assessed value under this paragraph from the prior year, whichever is greater.

(b) The assessed value of the property shall equal the lesser of:

(A) The real market value of the property reduced by the partial exemption; or

(B) The maximum assessed value of the property under paragraph (a) of this subsection.

(2) ***Unless determined under a provision of law governing the special assessment***, the maximum assessed value subject to special assessment and the assessed value of property subject to special assessment shall be determined as follows:

(a) The maximum assessed value:

(A) For the first tax year in which the property is specially assessed, shall equal the specially assessed value of the property multiplied by the ratio, not greater than 1.00, of the average maximum assessed value over the average real market value for the tax year of property in the same area and property class.

(B) For each tax year after the first tax year in which property is subject to the same special assessment, shall equal 103 percent of the property's assessed value for the prior year or 100 percent of the property's maximum assessed value subject to special assessment from the prior year, whichever is greater.

(b) The assessed value of the property shall equal the **lesser of:**

(A) The specially assessed value of the property *__as determined under the law establishing the special assessment__*; **or** (my note – see ORS 446.525)

(B) The property's maximum assessed value subject to special assessment as determined under paragraph (a) of this subsection.

(3) As used in this section, "area" and "property class" have the meanings given those terms in ORS 308.149. [2003 c.169 §6]

Yes, the tax laws are difficult to follow because applicable law is found in a multitude of Chapters. Regardless, the Department of Revenue employees and the Tax Courts are required to be competent – as previously noted. When an issue has been raised by a person there can be no defense of ignorance to mitigate criminal liability for the government public officers.

Yes, the assessors had in their files a statement of cost for my home (<u>Appendices E</u>) including add-on as $43,533. but the tax statement for 07/01/2002 To 06/30/2003 shows the RMV as $69,742. in   <u>(Appendices A</u>).That's a difference of $26,209. not identified on the tax statement as real property. This suggests that a deal was made to shift the tax liability from the land owner to my personal property and it increases the RMV for increase of future illegal tax collection. But they did lower the RMV to the purchase price of $43,000 after an appeal was submitted. This becomes very important because the manufactured structure <u>is tax</u> <u>exempt except for the $6. special assessment.</u>

To this point we've talked about the assessors, lawyers and the Board of Property Tax Appeals who have ***not complied*** with the applicable tax laws dealing with a <u>manufactured structure classified as personal property.</u>

Another issue of non-compliance is the increase of the assessed value (AV) that ***increased more than the allowed three percent every tax year since 2002***. But, bringing this to their attention falls on deaf ears with no reduction of the AV and <u>no criminal prosecution of the assessor.</u>

Constitution of Oregon , Article XI

Section 11. Property tax limitations on assessed value and rate of tax; exceptions. (1)(a) For the tax year beginning July 1, 1997, each unit of property in this state shall have a maximum assessed value for ad valorem property tax purposes that does not exceed the property's real market value for the tax year beginning July 1, 1995, reduced by 10 percent.

(b) For tax years beginning after July 1, 1997, the property's maximum assessed value **shall not increase by more than three percent from the previous tax year**.

The option of filing a civil suit would result in no accountability of the assessor who is the tax collector.

ORS 311.015 Recovery of damages and costs by person injured by false return or fraudulent act of tax collector. If a person is injured by the false return or ***fraudulent act of a tax collector***, such person shall recover upon suit, brought on the bond of the tax collector and sureties of the tax collector, double damages and costs of suit. [Amended by 1965 c.344 §9]

Chapter 8 - Board of Property Tax Appeals (BOPTA)

Usually a three member board that is required to take an oath to support the Constitution of Oregon and to faithfully serve (ORS 309.070)

They are employed by the Director Elizabeth Harchenko, Department of Revenue who is appointed by the Governor.

The County Clerks, Jan Coleman and Becky Stern Doll appointed County Counsel, John M. Gray, Jr. (his assistant is Rick Sanai) to act as legal counsel for BOPTA with authority under –

ORS 309.024 Record of proceedings; clerk; legal advisor; appraiser assistance. (1) The board of property tax appeals **_shall keep a written or audio record_** of all proceedings. Notwithstanding ORS 192.650, no written minutes need be made.

(2) The county clerk, as described in ORS 306.005, shall serve as clerk of the board. The clerk or deputy clerk shall attend sessions of the board at the discretion of the board as approved by the clerk.

(3) The district attorney or the county counsel, at the discretion of the county clerk, shall be the legal advisor of the board unless there is a potential conflict of interest in the district attorney or county counsel serving as the legal advisor. **_If there is a potential conflict of interest, the county clerk may appoint independent counsel to serve as the legal advisor of the board._** The legal advisor of the board, or the legal advisor's deputy, may attend all sessions of the board.

(4) At the discretion of the county clerk, the board may hire one or more appraisers registered under ORS 308.010, or licensed or certified under ORS 674.310, and not otherwise employed by the county, and other necessary personnel for the purpose of aiding the board in carrying out its functions and duties under ORS 309.026. The boards of the various counties may make such reciprocal arrangements for the exchange of appraisers with other counties as will most effectively carry out the functions and duties of the boards. [1953 c.714 §3; 1955 c.709 §3; 1957 c.326 §2; 1971 c.377 §2; 1973 c.336 §1; 1981 c.804 §2; 1989 c.330 §16; 1991 c.5 §24; 1991 c.459 §189; 1993 c.270 §40; 1993 c.498 §3; 1997 c.541 §225a; 2001 c.511 §2; 2005 c.94 §59]

Appeals for redress from illegal taxation are usually filed before December 31 following the tax assessment.

In a constitutional environment of compliance this would have been resolved with the assessor; however, this did not happen.

An appeal from the assessor's decision goes to the BOPTA for compliance with applicable law.

If you disagree with the BOPTA decision – further appeals may be filed in the Tax Courts – Magistrate division then to the Regular division.

Further appeal to the Supreme Court has a limited purpose because the Legislature has given the Tax Court power to decide a tax issue in ORS 305.410 (4). Yes, it is a travesty that the Legislature decided to give the Tax Court oligarchal, dictatorship powers unless an issue is filed with the Supreme Court who has final jurisdiction to decide the *facts and applicable law.*

ORS 305.410 Authority of court in tax cases within its jurisdiction; concurrent jurisdiction; exclusive jurisdiction in certain cases.
(1) Subject only to the provisions of ORS 305.445 relating to judicial review by the Supreme Court and to subsection (2) of this section, the tax court shall be the sole, exclusive and final judicial authority for the hearing and determination of all questions of law and fact arising under the tax laws of this state. For the purposes of this section, and except to the extent that they preclude the imposition of other taxes, the following are not tax laws of this state:

(a) ORS chapter 577 relating to Oregon Beef Council contributions.

(b) ORS 576.051 to 576.455 relating to commodity commission assessments.

(c) ORS chapter 477 relating to fire protection assessments.

(d) ORS chapters 731, 732, 733, 734, 737, 742, 743, 743A, 744, 746, 748 and 750 relating to insurance company fees and taxes.

(e) ORS chapter 473 relating to liquor taxes.

(f) ORS chapter 583 relating to milk marketing, production or distribution fees.

(g) ORS chapter 825 relating to motor carrier taxes.

(h) ORS chapter 319 relating to motor vehicle and aircraft fuel taxes.

(i) ORS title 59 relating to motor vehicle and motor vehicle operators' license fees and ORS title 39 relating to boat licenses.

(j) ORS chapter 578 relating to Oregon Wheat Commission assessments.

(k) ORS chapter 462 relating to racing taxes.

(L) ORS chapter 657 relating to unemployment insurance taxes.

(m) ORS chapter 656 relating to workers' compensation contributions, assessments or fees.

(n) ORS 311.420, 311.425, 311.455, 311.650, 311.655 and ORS chapter 312 relating to foreclosure of real and personal property tax liens.

(o) Sections 15 to 22, chapter 736, Oregon Laws 2003, relating to long term care facility assessments.

(2) The tax court and the circuit courts shall have concurrent jurisdiction to try actions or suits to determine:

(a) The priority of property tax liens in relation to other liens.

(b) The validity of any deed, conveyance, transfer or assignment of real or personal property under ORS 95.060 and 95.070 (1983 Replacement Part) or 95.200 to 95.310 where the Department of Revenue has or claims a lien or other interest in the property.

(3) Subject only to the provisions of ORS 305.445 relating to judicial review by the Supreme Court, the tax court shall be the sole, exclusive and final judicial authority for the hearing and determination of all questions of law and fact concerning the authorized uses of the proceeds of bonded indebtedness described in section 11 (11)(d), Article XI of the Oregon Constitution.

(4) **Except as permitted under section 2, amended Article VII, Oregon Constitution, this section and ORS 305.445**, no person shall contest, in any action, suit or proceeding in the circuit court or any other court, any matter within the jurisdiction of the tax court. [1961 c.533 §12; 1965 c.6 §2; 1967 c.359 §688; 1969 c.48 §1; 1971 c.567 §14; 1975 c.365 §1; 1977 c.407 §1; 1985 c.149 §5; 1985 c.664 §18; 2003 c.195 §18; 2003 c.604 §100; 2007 c.780 §29]

The Supreme Court has other additional authorities and responsibilities to hold Tax Court judges accountable.

Chapter 9 - Oregon Code of Judicial Conduct and Oregon Code of Professional Conduct

Within the statute ORS 9.490 the Supreme Court "shall have power to enforce" implies a responsibility to punish misconduct. The Code(s) are not herein duplicated but they are available on the internet. The judges are usually lawyers – both Code(s) apply.

ORS 9.490 Formulation of rules of professional conduct; prohibition on certain sanctions for violation of rule. (1) The board of governors, with the approval of the house of delegates given at any regular or special meeting, shall formulate rules of professional conduct, and when such rules are adopted by the Supreme Court, ***shall have power to enforce the same***. <u>Such rules shall be binding upon all members of the bar.</u>

(2) A court of this state may not order that evidence be suppressed or excluded in any criminal trial, grand jury proceeding or other criminal proceeding, or order that any criminal prosecution be dismissed, solely as a sanction or remedy for violation of a rule of professional conduct adopted by the Supreme Court. [Amended by 1995 c.302 §19; 1995 c.708 §2]

ORS 9.010 Status of attorney and Oregon State Bar; applicability of statutes. (1) An attorney, admitted to practice in this state, ***is an officer of the court.***

ORS 9.460 Duties of attorneys. *An attorney shall:*

43

(1) Support the Constitution and laws of the United States **and of this state;**

(2) Employ, for the purpose of maintaining the causes confided to the attorney, such means only as are consistent with truth, and never seek to mislead the court or jury by any artifice or false statement of law or fact;

(3) Maintain the confidences and secrets of the attorney's clients consistent with the rules of professional conduct established pursuant to ORS 9.490; and

(4) Never reject, for any personal consideration, the cause of the defenseless or the oppressed. [Amended by 1989 c.1052 §9; 1991 c.726 §5]

ORS 9.310 Attorney defined; counsel. An attorney is a person authorized to represent a party in the written proceedings in any action, suit or proceeding, in any stage thereof. An attorney, other than the one who represents the party in the written proceedings, may also represent a party in court, or before a judicial officer, in which case the attorney is known as counsel, and the authority of the attorney is limited to the matters that transpire in the court or before such officer at the time.

Notice that the word "may" is used in ORS 9.527. As a consequence a lawyer or judge most probably will never be held accountable for their criminal acts – misdemeanors or felonies.

ORS 9.527 Grounds for disbarment, suspension or reprimand. The Supreme Court *__may__* disbar, suspend or reprimand a member of the bar whenever, upon proper proceedings for that purpose, it appears to the court that:

(1) The member has committed an act or carried on a course of conduct of such nature that, if the member were applying for admission to the bar, the application should be denied;

(2) The member has been convicted in any jurisdiction of an offense which is a misdemeanor involving moral turpitude or a felony under

the laws of this state, or is punishable by death or imprisonment under the laws of the United States, in any of which cases the record of the conviction shall be conclusive evidence;

(3) The member has willfully disobeyed an order of a court requiring the member to do or forbear an act connected with the legal profession;

(4) The member is guilty of willful deceit or misconduct in the legal profession;

(5) The member is guilty of willful violation of any of the provisions of ORS 9.460 or 9.510;

(6) The member is guilty of gross or repeated negligence or incompetence in the practice of law; or

(7) The member has violated any of the provisions of the rules of professional conduct adopted pursuant to ORS 9.490. [Formerly 9.480; 1989 c.1052 §11]

Oregon Code of Judicial Conduct are the rules that hold accountable (maybe) a judge's behavior on and off the bench.

JR 1 – 101 (B) A judge shall not commit a criminal act.

JR 1 – 101 (D) A judge shall not engage in conduct involving dishonesty, fraud, deceit or misrepresentation.

JR 2 – 104 requires a judge report another judge if that judge has violated any of the code

JR 2 – 106 says that a judge shall disqualify himself or herself when the judge has a bias or prejudice

JR 2 – 107 A judge shall be faithful to the law and shall decide matters on the basis of the ***facts and applicable law***.

These Judicial Rules (JR) are in fact law authorized by the statute cited above – ORS 9.490.

Code of Professional Conduct
Rule 3.3 Candor Toward the Tribunal

(a) A lawyer shall not <u>knowingly</u>:

(1) make a false statement of fact or law to a <u>tribunal</u> ***or fail to correct a false statement of material fact or law previously made to the tribunal by the lawyer;***

The reproductions above are just a tip of the iceberg of applicable code. The Supreme Court with the Legislature intended that the Justice system must be honest and transparent. However, if transgressions are not prosecuted – then none of it is worth the paper it's printed on.

Tyranny and insurrection is the triumphant victor.

Chapter 10 - Tax Court – Magistrate and Regular Division

Creation of the Tax Court can be found in ORS 305.404 and ORS 305.405. The Legislature has given the Supreme Court limited review authority under ORS 305.445 and ORS 305.410 (4); however, the Chief Justice has other authorities and responsibilities to hold the Tax Court judges accountable.

This created an oligarchal dictatorship in the Tax Court with impertinence for dishonesty, deceit, fraud, misrepresentation of laws, abusive power, intimidation, dissemination of court decisions with intent to discredit the Plaintiff, and wrongful interpretation of the frivolous law.

> **ORS 305.404 Oregon Tax Court; definitions; usage.** Unless the context requires otherwise, as used in ORS 305.404 to 305.560 and other revenue and tax laws, "tax court" or "Oregon Tax Court" means the Oregon Tax Court created under ORS 305.405. In an appropriate case, "tax court" may include either the regular division or the magistrate division of the Oregon Tax Court, or both, or the judge or judges of the tax court or its magistrates or a combination. In a few instances, "tax court" may include the tax court clerk or other employees of the regular or magistrate division of the tax court. [1995 c.650 §104]

> **ORS 305.405 Oregon Tax Court; creation; jurisdiction.** As part of the judicial branch of state government, there is created a court of justice to be known as the Oregon Tax Court. The tax court, in cases within its jurisdiction pursuant to ORS 305.410:

(1) Is a court of record and of general jurisdiction, not limited, special or inferior jurisdiction.

(2) <u>Has the same powers as a circuit court.</u>

(3) Has and may exercise all ordinary and extraordinary legal, equitable and provisional remedies available in the circuit courts, as well as such additional remedies as may be assigned to it. [1961 c.533 §1; 1965 c.6 §1]

ORS 305.410 Authority of court in tax cases within its jurisdiction; concurrent jurisdiction; exclusive jurisdiction in certain cases. (1) ***Subject only*** to the provisions of ORS 305.445 relating ***to judicial review by the Supreme Court*** and to subsection (2) of this section, the tax court shall be the sole, exclusive and final judicial authority for the hearing and determination of all questions of law and fact arising under the tax laws of this state. For the purposes of this section, and except to the extent that they preclude the imposition of other taxes, the following are not tax laws of this state:

(a) ORS chapter 577 relating to Oregon Beef Council contributions.

(b) ORS 576.051 to 576.455 relating to commodity commission assessments.

(c) ORS chapter 477 relating to fire protection assessments.

(d) ORS chapters 731, 732, 733, 734, 737, 742, 743, 743A, 744, 746, 748 and 750 relating to insurance company fees and taxes.

(e) ORS chapter 473 relating to liquor taxes.

(f) ORS chapter 583 relating to milk marketing, production or distribution fees.

(g) ORS chapter 825 relating to motor carrier taxes.

(h) ORS chapter 319 relating to motor vehicle and aircraft fuel taxes.

(i) ORS title 59 relating to motor vehicle and motor vehicle operators' license fees and ORS title 39 relating to boat licenses.

(j) ORS chapter 578 relating to Oregon Wheat Commission assessments.

(k) ORS chapter 462 relating to racing taxes.

(L) ORS chapter 657 relating to unemployment insurance taxes.

(m) ORS chapter 656 relating to workers' compensation contributions, assessments or fees.

(n) ORS 311.420, 311.425, 311.455, 311.650, 311.655 and ORS chapter 312 relating to foreclosure of real and personal property tax liens.

(o) Sections 15 to 22, chapter 736, Oregon Laws 2003, relating to long term care facility assessments.

(2) The tax court and the circuit courts shall have concurrent jurisdiction to try actions or suits to determine:

(a) The priority of property tax liens in relation to other liens.

(b) The validity of any deed, conveyance, transfer or assignment of real or personal property under ORS 95.060 and 95.070 (1983 Replacement Part) or 95.200 to 95.310 where the Department of Revenue has or claims a lien or other interest in the property.

(3) Subject only to the provisions of ORS 305.445 relating to judicial review by the Supreme Court, the tax court shall be the sole, exclusive and final judicial authority for the hearing and determination of all questions of law and fact concerning the authorized uses of the proceeds of bonded indebtedness described in section 11 (11)(d), Article XI of the Oregon Constitution.

(4) ***Except as permitted under section 2, amended Article VII, Oregon Constitution, this section and ORS 305.445***, no person

shall contest, in any action, suit or proceeding in the circuit court or any other court, any matter within the jurisdiction of the tax court. [1961 c.533 §12; 1965 c.6 §2; 1967 c.359 §688; 1969 c.48 §1; 1971 c.567 §14; 1975 c.365 §1; 1977 c.407 §1; 1985 c.149 §5; 1985 c.664 §18; 2003 c.195 §18; 2003 c.604 §100; 2007 c.780 §29]

The imposition of a maximum frivolous penalty (TC 4767) was, unquestionable, **intended to deter any other appeals _on the issue of illegal taxation of personal property_**. Unfortunately I have found no legal definition of "objectively reasonable" thus leaving the definition to mean whatever convoluted meaning the tax court judge wants to give.

ORS 305.437 Damages for frivolous or groundless appeal or appeal to delay. (1) **_Whenever it appears to the Oregon Tax Court_** that proceedings before it have been instituted or maintained by a taxpayer primarily for delay or that the taxpayer's position in such proceeding is frivolous or groundless, damages in an amount not to exceed $5,000 shall be awarded to the Department of Revenue by the Oregon Tax Court in its judgment. Damages so awarded shall be paid within 10 days after the judgment becomes final. If the damages remain unpaid, the department may collect the amount awarded in the same manner as income taxes are collected under ORS 314.430.

(2) As used in this section, **a taxpayer's position is "frivolous" if there was no objectively reasonable basis for asserting the position.** [1987 c.843 §4; 1995 c.650 §6a]

Read carefully the decisions that were splashed across the internet. The decisions are rife with violations of the Code(s) :

Gall v Department of Revenue : TC – MD 060207C ; TC 4767 posted under November 20, 2006(3 entries)

SC – S54580 posted under 10-11-07(TC 4767)

TC – MD030131B ; TC 4639 posted July 12, 2004 ; SC – S51473 posted under 9-30-04(TC 4639)

Keep in mind that the court ***does not publish the motions*** filed by the Plaintiff/Appellant. To get a clear picture of any court case you must take the time to read the entire record.

Don't assume the court decision has complied with the mandate to decide on the <u>facts and the law.</u>

The records a available as noted in ORS 305.485.

> **ORS 305.485 Records.** (1) The records of the tax court shall include a register, journal and fee book.
>
> (2) The register is a book wherein the clerk shall enter, by its title, every suit or proceeding commenced in, or transferred or appealed to, the tax court, according to the date of its commencement, transfer or appeal. Thereafter, until the entry of judgment, the clerk shall note therein, according to the date thereof, the filing or return of any paper or process, or the making of any order, rule or other direction in or concerning such suit or proceeding.
>
> (3) The journal is a book wherein the clerk shall enter the proceedings of the court.
>
> (4) The fee book is a book wherein the clerk shall enter, under the title of every cause, against the party to whom the service is rendered, the clerk's fees earned, and whether received or not received.
>
> (5) The files of the court are all papers or process filed with or by the clerk of the court, in any suit or proceeding therein, or before the judge.
>
> (6) Separate records shall be kept for the magistrate division.
>
> (7) ORS 7.095, authorizing the use of electronic data processing techniques, is applicable to the records required by this section. [1961 c.533 §10; 1995 c.273 §26; 1995 c.650 §5; 1997 c.325 §§9,10]

When reading the record you will notice that many, many issues were raised – the following is just one ! The introduction by Defendant of the word "additional" to change the meaning of ORS 446.525 was a violation of the Code. The judge should have known but did not reject the statement thus it became the entire basis to perpetuate the illegal taxation.

And, in the TRANSCRIPT OF PROCEEDINGS prepared by Velma Foster, Transcriber of TC 4767 dated September 21, 2006 on page 2 starting on line 13 Judge Breithaupt refers to Defendant's Trial Memorandum that both plaintiff and defendant stipulated an agreement to proceed – fast forward to page 4 line 1 thru 4 to notice that MR. ADAIR the attorney for defendant made a dishonest statement " the Yamhill County Assessor assessed plaintiff's manufactured structure as personal property". Then on line 5 MR GALL states " Not correct " but the judge moved on ignoring the lie. Then the judge repeats the lie on line 12 thru 15. At this point the judge should have declared that attorney Adair had violated the law in Rule 3.3 Candor Toward the Tribunal and other law and proceeded to report Adair to the Oregon State Bar. But that didn't happen. The judge went on with the trial to violate other laws.

(TC 4796; SC S055852) *19 OTR 398 (2008).

BALMER, J.

We agree that a judicial or agency rule that conflicts with a statute is invalid to the extent that it so conflicts and that a rule created within a statutory scheme cannot amend, alter, enlarge upon, or limit statutory wording so that it has the effect of undermining the legislative intent. *See Miller v. Employment Division*, **290 Or 285, 289, 620 P2d 1377 (1980) ("An agency may not amend, alter, enlarge or limit the terms of a legislative enactment by rule."**

http://bluebook.state.or.us/state/judicial/judicial28.htm
Cases Filed in Oregon Courts: 2000-2007

Court	2000	2001	2002	2003	2004	2005	2006	2007
Oregon Supreme Court	1,004	1,018	939	1,028	999	1,062	1,347	1,274
Oregon Court of Appeals	4,073	4,297	3,277	3,314	3,677	3,801	3,517	3,317
Tax Court -Regular Division	78	32	47	55	39	43	27	26
Tax Court - Magistrate Division	1,200	1,186	1,245	1,047	1,184	1,021	827	915
Circuit Courts	653,367	654,822	645,956	655,574	607,539	611,946	602,896	605,753

Note:

Data on Supreme Court filings includes petitions for review and original proceedings filed. This is a change from previous statistics and is reflected in the 2000–2007 statistics.

Notice that the reduction before the Tax Court Regular Division is almost 70% and is addressed in my MOTION to waive rules for good cause and to review En Banc.

The MOTION exposed a direct threat made by Judge Breithaupt. This motion was denied by the Supreme Court.

As a Christian we understand that final judgment is not of this earth life.

My reading of the Bible tells me that restitution must be made to receive forgiveness and eternal salvation.

The BILL OF RIGHTS , Article I says the " Congress shall make no law respecting an establishment of religion ", so – you're free to believe otherwise.

Chapter 11 - Supreme Court

Although this court has limited review authority of a tax issue as pointed out in the previous Chapter. The reality is something different. But, how many lawyers would dig deeper to competently represent a client?

If we look deep into the laws governing tax and other issues a fact is that we need deep pockets to jump through the hoops and over the hurdles unless public officers respect their oath.

To understand what I mean we need to examine some laws that would have a person believe that the end of an appeal resides in the tax court but ORS 305.410 (4) disputes this.

First we need to look at the Constitution of Oregon, Article IV,

> **Section 21. Acts to be plainly worded.** Every act, and joint resolution shall be plainly worded, avoiding as far as practicable the use of technical terms.–

Then take a look at Article VII (Amended)

> **Section 2. Amendment's effect on courts, jurisdiction and judicial system; Supreme Court's original jurisdiction.** The courts, jurisdiction, and judicial system of Oregon, except so far as expressly changed by this amendment, shall remain as at present constituted until otherwise provided by law. But the supreme court may, in its own discretion, take original jurisdiction *in mandamus, quo warranto and habeas corpus proceedings*. [Created through initiative petition filed July 7, 1910, and adopted by the people Nov. 8, 1910]

WHY? Did the Legislature use legal terms in Section 2. ?? Plain language could have been used to convey the intent.

Law Dictionary –

Mandamus : A **writ of mandamus** or simply *mandamus*, which means "we command" in Latin, is the name of one of the prerogative writs in the common law, and is issued by a superior court to compel a lower court or a government officer to perform mandatory or purely ministerial duties correctly.[1]

Quo warranto (Medieval Latin for "by what warrant?") is a prerogative writ requiring the person to whom it is directed to show what authority he has for exercising some right or power (or "franchise") he claims to hold.

Habeas Corpus, literally in Latin "you have the body" is a term that represents an important right granted to individuals in America. Basically, a writ of habeas corpus is a judicial mandate requiring that a prisoner be brought before the court to determine whether the government has the right to continue detaining them. The individual being held or their representative can petition the court for such a writ.

According to Article One of the Constitution, the right to a writ of habeas corpus can only be suspended "in cases of rebellion or invasion the public safety." Habeas corpus was suspended during the Civil War and Reconstruction, in parts of South Carolina during the fight against the Ku Klux Klan, and during the War on Terror

habeas corpus definition

ha·beas cor·pus (hā′bē əs kôr′pəs)

Law any of various writs ordering a person to be brought before a court; specif., a writ requiring that a detained person be brought before a court to decide the legality of the detention or imprisonment

in full habeas corpus ad subjiciendum habeas corpus ad′· sub·ji′·ci·en′·dum (ad′ sub jis′ē en′dəm)

We see in mandamus that the Supreme Court could have, *on its own motion*, taken original jurisdiction to invoke their superior judicial position to initiate a mandamus *to enforce the law as it relates to the facts and applicable law*. But, that did not happen!

At this time I must repeat that **I am not a lawyer.** Eight years of research and petitioning for redress has revealed many violations of law, perpetrated by public officers, reaching the level of Class B Felonies

This court ignored my requests contained in the BRIEF as Relief Sought. <u>One of those requests was to cease-and-desist the illegal taxation of my personal property</u>, a manufactured structure, sited on rented land. Other requests were not honored nor addressed in this court's decisions.***Contrary to the facts and applicable law this court affirmed the lower court decision***. A reasonable person could conclude that Supreme Court Justice W. Michael Gillette (SC – S51473) and Justice Rives Kistler (SC – S54580) wrote their decisions without ever reading the record; specifically, I believe the decisions were written by court clerks (lawyers). But, the Justices are ultimately responsible and accountable.

Because this court has not taken affirmative action it is derelict and has aided-and-abetted the perpetuation of the theft and extortion by the Executive and Tax Courts (see Chapter 6 – ORS 161.155).

Without doubt, this court had a legal obligation to exercise the option within the mandates of ORS 162.415 (see Chapter 5 – Accountability). This highlights the corruption in government at the highest levels.

If you are so inclined you will find, in the record, court ordered denials of legitimate plaintiff/appellant motions. You will find some included here in the Appendices.

What did the court mean – dismissed as moot? A legal definition is much different than a normal understanding.

moot definition

moot (mo‾o‾t)

noun

an early English assembly of freemen to administer justice, decide community problems, etc.

a discussion or argument, esp. of a hypothetical law case, as in a law school

Etymology: ME *mote* < OE *mot, gemot,* a meeting & prob. ON *mot* < Gmc base **mot-* > Goth *gamotjan,* to meet

adjective
1. subject to or open for discussion or debate; debatable
2. not worthy of consideration or discussion because it has been resolved or no longer needs to be resolved

transitive verb
1. to debate or discuss
2. to propose or bring up for discussion or debate
3. to make so hypothetical as to deprive of significance; make academic or theoretical

To debate or discuss or has been resolved ? ? The purpose for the petitions for redress of grievances were submitted for the courts to resolve.

But the questions have not been resolved according to the facts and applicable law (see Chapter 9, JR 2 -107).

The foregoing revelations are not the whole story but to include herein all the motions filed by me would be redundant.

However, two of the most recent are included to give you a better understanding of the process.

The first of these is <u>Appendices G</u> APPELLANT's MOTION – Reconsider Order dated January 07, 2009;

The second is in <u>Appendices K</u>, MOTION to waive rules for good cause and
to review En Banc;
Notice that Mr. Adair did not recant any statements of record.

Additionally, <u>Appendices P</u>, shows that my appeals have solicited involvement
of the Dean and Professor of Law, Dean Symeonides of the Willamette University
College of Law - because some of the adjunct faculty included Supreme Court
Justices and Tax Court Judge Breithaupt.

You need to know that I have reason to believe that Dean Symeonides and Chief
Justice De Muniz are honorable men.

Unfortunately, the wheels of justice roll much to slow to satisfy a victim of
government tyranny.

Chapter 12   -   Governor

Finally, there are indicators that Governor Kulongoski has responded to my **third** letter that was mailed certified with return receipt requested. But he did not reply as requested. The letter is included herein as <u>Appendices Q</u>.

One indicator is the 2009-2010 PERSONAL PROPERTY PETITION , Form 150-310-064 (Rev. 09-09) with its attached instruction for filing, the first paragraph, that states <u>***"Personal property is taxable in Oregon if it is currently being used or being held for use in a business, or is floating property".***</u>

But, the Governor did not issue an order to his appointed Director Harchenko, Department of Revenue to obey the tax laws of this State <u>***or she is disobeying his orders.***</u> This is apparent because the Yamhill County assessor/tax collector again sent assessments to owners of **personal property that is exempt** (except for the $6. that could be collected by the Director of the Housing and Community Services Department as authorized under ORS 446.525 (4).

The illegal tax assessments are theft and extortion discussed in Chapter 7 (ORS 164.075); nonetheless, the Tax Statement **threatens** to seize the home and garnish other financial assets if the assessments are not paid .

Surely the Governor knows that personal property is protected under The BILL OF RIGHTS, Article IV and Article IX and Article X.

If the Governor followed the Constitution of Oregon, Article V, Section 10. he would have ordered the State Police to supervise the actions of the Director and assessors.

The Governor's biography posted on the internet suggests that he knows the court precedent cited in Chapter 6 and Chapter 10; and he should know this one :

"An unconstitutional act is not law; it confers no rights; it imposes no duties; affords no protection; it creates no office; it is in legal contemplation, as inoperative as though it had never been passed."

Norton vs. Shelby County

118 US 425 p. 442

If the Governor recognizes court precedent as law – then he will instruct his appointed Director to ignore ORS 306.220 (4) because in this case the Tax Court Judge Breithaupt is guilty of an unconstitutional act when he affirmed the assessor's illegal actions and set a fine of $5,000.00 under ORS 305.437 the frivolous statute.

> **ORS 306.220 Compliance of public officers with laws and orders affecting property taxes.** (1) *__Every public officer shall comply with any lawful order__*, rule or regulation of the Department of Revenue made under ORS 306.115, 308.335 or 309.400.
>
> (2) Whenever it appears to the department that any public officer or employee whose duties relate to the assessment or equalization of assessments of property for taxation has failed to comply with any law relating to such duties, or the rules of the department made in pursuance thereof, the department, after an informal conference on the facts, may direct the public officer or employee to comply with such law or rule.
>
> (3) If the public officer or employee, for a period of 10 days after service on the public officer or employee of the department's direction, neglects or refuses to comply therewith, the department may apply to the Oregon Tax Court for an order, returnable within five days from the date thereof, to compel the public officer or employee to comply with the law or rule, or to show cause why the public officer or employee should not be compelled so to do.
>
> (4) Any order issued by the judge pursuant thereto shall be final.
>
> (5) The remedy provided in this section shall be cumulative and shall not preclude the department from exercising any power or rights delegated to it. [Amended by 1983 c.605 §4; 1993 c.18 §67; 1995 c.650 §69; 1999 c.21 §13]

As a consequence, the Governor has "Criminal liability for conduct of another" as stated in ORS 161.155 (see Chapter 6) and ORS 164.075 (h) (see Chapter 7).

It got worse! According to the Associated Press , on Saturday,
May 9, 2009 "Gov. Ted Kulongoski has named the U.S. Attorney for Oregon,
Karin Immergut, as a state judge in Multnomah County."

This explained why the U.S. Attorney's office refused to act on
my report of Oregon corruption – refusing to enforce The CONSTITUTION
OF THE UNITED STATES, Article IV, Section 4.

"The United States shall guarantee to every State in this Union a Republican Form of Government,". . .

Apparently Karin Immergut had no stomach to prosecute a Governor who "had teamed up with Kulongoski on several law enforcement issues".

There is more! The News-Register reported "Governor appoints Easterday Yamhill County Judge".

After leaving the district attorney's office,
 Easterday went to work from July 2006 – November 2007 for the
Oregon State Bar, in the Client Assistance Office.
She investigated and reviewed ethical complaints against lawyers.

The appointment of Easterday followed my reports to the Oregon State Bar of judges and lawyers malfeasance.

These two appointments just don't pass the smell test.

Chapter 13 - *public servant incompetence and / or malfeasance*

Appendices P is a letter to five addressees soliciting support to expose many recalcitrant employees in Oregon government – to seek appropriate disbarment – and to seek removal from office the judges who have aided and abetted the prevalent insurrection.

As of this writing it is unknown whether anyone has been criminally prosecuted for their misconduct.

Chapter 14 - media / press

The media and the press have been a total disappointment. Although they have no obligation to respond to a citizen request, they do have an ethical responsibility, as a journalist, to expose government corruption.

Perhaps this book would be unnecessary if a journalist had been willing to cooperate; and, the reporting would be grammatically correct.

This is a link to information that may be of interest to you.

<u>CODE OF ETHICS</u>

Journalists should: —Avoid conflicts of interest, real or perceived.

— Remain free of associations and activities that may compromise integrity or damage credibility.

— Refuse gifts, favors, fees, free travel and special treatment, and shun secondary employment, political involvement, public office and service in community organizations if they compromise journalistic integrity.

— Disclose unavoidable conflicts.

— **<u>Be vigilant and courageous about holding those with power accountable.</u>**

— Deny favored treatment to advertisers and special interests and resist their pressure to influence news coverage.

— Be wary of sources offering information for favors or money; avoid bidding for news.
quote from Society of Professional Journalists
http://www.spj.org/ethicscode.asp

Chapter 15   -   take back our government

Yes, we can take back our government if we form a citizen movement to act in accordance with the Constitution of Oregon,   Article I,

> **Section 1. Natural rights inherent in people.** We declare that all men, when they form a social compact are equal in right: that all power is inherent in the people, and all free governments are founded on their authority, and instituted for their peace, safety, and happiness; and they have at all times a right to alter, reform, or abolish the government **in such manner as they may think proper.–**

This authorizes a citizen movement to control or remove the existing government but it doesn't say anything about making it simple or swift; however, this Constitution provides a pathway via amendments by initiative petition authorized in: Article XVII,

> **Section 1. Method of amending Constitution.**

> This article shall not be construed to impair the right of the people to amend this Constitution by vote upon an initiative petition therefor. [Created through initiative petition filed Feb. 3, 1906, and adopted by the people June 4, 1906]

That said, any movement would require an organization to gather the required signatures to place an initiative petition before the people for passage. This would not be easy. The cost would necessitate a person with deep pockets.

Another obstacle would be the push-back by those in government who would not want to subject themselves to control by the people.

To succeed, an organization would need an energetic leader who is dedicated to advance an impartial constitutional agenda.

The previous Chapters have shown that neither the Justice Department nor the Yamhill County District Attorney – neither of them prosecuted anyone associated with the illegal taxation. If they had, it would have been published with big headlines. I saw none !

An initiative petition must include language to **remove sole <u>criminal prosecutorial power</u>** from the government.

The following suggestions could be rewritten to become more stringent law.

SUBJ ;   requesting : amend, repeal, add

1.   **Amend** Constitution of Oregon , Article VII (Amended), Judicial Department
Section 6. incompetency or malfeasance of public officer. Public officers shall not be impeached; but incompetency, corruption, malfeasance or delinquency in office [- may -] [+ **shall** +] be tried in the same manner as criminal offenses, and judgment [- may -]
[+ **shall** +] be given of dismissal from office, and such further punishment as may have been prescribed by law. [Created through initiative petition filed July 7, 1910, and adopted by the people
Nov. 8, 1910]

2.   **Amend** the Constitution of Oregon, Article IV -

Section 24. **Suit against state.** Provision [- may -] [+ shall +] be made by general law, for bringing suit against the State, as to all liabilities originating after, or existing at the time of the adoption of this Constitution; but no special act authorizeing [sic] such suit to be brought, or making compensation to any person claiming damages against the State, [+ except when a State public officer has committed a criminal act +] , shall ever be passed.

3.   **repeal** Oregon Revised Statute(s) to preserve the Separation of Powers.

ORS 18.035 thru 18.052

SUBJ: Suggesting – petition - referendum: **add**
Constitution of OREGON
ARTICLE I
BILL OF RIGHTS

Section 46. **Rights reserved for the people; right to prosecute.**
In consort with ARTICLE I, Section 1. and ARTICLE VII(Amended), Section 6. of this Constitution and when in the interest of justice, the right to prosecute criminal malfeasance of a public officer shall remain inviolate with the people of this State. Any person of this State may bring charges before a court of this State authorized to hear a criminal case

before a jury of State residents – and, may be <u>assisted </u>by a lawyer who is authorized to practice in this or any other State. Reprisal or any attempt of reprisal shall be prosecuted as a Class B Felony. This Section shall become effective upon passage by the people irrespective of Article IV, Section 28 of this Constitution.

Section 47. Rights reserved for the people; right to prosecute.

In consort with Section 1. of this Constitution the people of this State do hereby limit the authorities of Congress and other entities of government. No tax, fee or assessment shall be imposed upon the people of this State unless first approved by the people by ballot. The ballot language shall be simple without deceit nor fraudulent misrepresentations. Violations of this Article shall be tried in court as authorized by Article VII(Amended) Section 6. before a jury and punishment shall be as a Class B Felony. Prosecution may be brought before a criminal trial court by any person who is a resident of this State and may be assisted by a lawyer of this State or any other State. This Section shall become effective upon passage by the people irrespective of Article IV, Section 28 of this Constitution.

Chapter 16   -   Government: What is it? For what purpose?

What is it? It is whatever the people allow within the confines of the Constitution of Oregon.

We elect some of the public officers but others are appointed by those we elect. This is the reason we must educate ourselves about those who campaign for a government office. Always, we must ask – what is their agenda and who is supporting the campaign?

We get a government of rogue public officers if our attention is focused on acceptance of the redistribution of private property (money). These rogue public officers have an insatiable appetite for our money to support their affluent lifestyle during their employment and into their retirement years. These rogue public officers have no respect for a constitutional Republican Form of government.

So, we the people must examine our own conscience to decide the form of government we want to serve us. If we decide to allow an arrogant dictatorship then that is what we will have. If you demand a government of law then you will be free to exercise all rights preserved in the BILL OF RIGHTS and the Constitution of Oregon.

If we elect as Governor a dishonest person then all of government will be dishonest because no public servant will be held accountable.

No accountability = corruption !

For what purpose is government? The purpose is to provide a service – hence, public servants.

In 1995 government was given a mandate, passed by the people, to prioritize public safety and education. This is stated in Measure 50 but it is largely ignored by our public servants.

Whenever there is a shortfall of your money in government coffers the public servants plead for more taxes to shore-up the State Police and the government public education system.

Of course this tactic is dishonest, deceitful and misrepresents the will of the people as mandated in Measure 50.

I submit that an honest government would manage the budget in the same way we must manage our own money – ***save for a rainy day.***

Yes, this means **<u>less social welfare</u>** to encourage personal accountability and to encourage **<u>less waste in government</u>** as they provide the services we have come to expect.

Chapter 17 - Summary

This exposure of corruption is intended to cull the rotten apples. Any farmer can tell you that one rotten apple will soon ruin the entire bushel if it isn't thrown out. So too we must cull the rotten public servants from government with your informed vote at the ballot box.

This exposure is **not intended** to disparage the thousands of honest hard working public servants who give a days work for a days wages. And, we appreciate those who have made it possible for us to GOOGLE government documents. We the People should, on bended knee, give thanks that thousands have served honorably despite corrupt leadership.

Within these pages are many references to the Oregon Revised Statute(s) (ORS) so that you, the interested reader, can make a personal determination without a bias. Hopefully the ORS and Appendices are presented with a sensible pathway for understanding.

The illegal tax assessments were so irrational they had to be challenged with determination regardless of an unknown outcome. The taxation was perpetuated with a confidence that no trailer-trash would have a naïve expectation to successfully compel compliance with Oregon law.

Appendices R - is a letter from Director, Department of Revenue, Elizabeth Harchenko. This letter is an example of elitest, verbose, convoluted attempt to deceive , to misrepresent the applicable law. Its interesting that she too would point out that I did not get a lawyer to represent me. She is a lawyer, a member of the Oregon State Bar and an Officer of the Court who should know that an honest lawyer would not attempt to represent my cause against the State.

Appendices S - is the GENERAL JUDGMENT written by the Defendant attorney Adair. This is another example of law violations perpetrated by a lawyer and a judge. The Constitution of Oregon, Article III, Section 1.Separation of Powers takes precedence over the Oregon Revised Statute that authorized this action; however, Adair and Judge Breithaupt should have known this or be subject to prosecution for incompetency. This judgment is a blatant example of collusion to threaten anyone who would consider filing for redress in the tax court.

Section 1. Separation of powers. The powers of the Government shall be divided into three seperate [sic] departments, the Legislative, the Executive, including the administrative, and the Judicial; and **no person charged with official duties under one of these departments**, shall exercise any of the functions of another, except as in **this Constitution** expressly provided.–

Appendices T - my letter dated March 2009 to Chief Justice Paul J. DeMuniz via Dean Symeonides is another appeal for justice.

Appendices U - my letter dated November 30, 2009 to Chief Justice Paul J. DeMuniz and Dean Symeonides raises questions of forgery, interference with the judicial process and the status of Justice W. Michael Gillette.

Appendices V and V-1 - raises a curious question. WHY did the assessor lower the assessed value (AV) so dramatically to $28,105. and then increase it by .9259 % ? ? This violated existing law in two ways: 1)   it ignored the special assessment classification and 2) it raised the AV above the 3 % allowed by Measure 50. But, more egregious is the affirmation by BOPTA who is mandated to enforce the law. COLLUSION ? ABSOLUTELY !

Appendices W - is a map showing Oregon counties and the number of mobile home spaces in each county. The computations at the bottom of the page are my guesstimates.

Appendices X - the 2009-10 Tax Statement is included to show that the current assessor / tax collector, Scott Maytubby, continues in the path of former assessor David Lawson. This assessment ignores the special assessment classification and the 3 % limit . These assessors have stated that they are in compliance with the court decisions; however, the court decisions are invalid as we have learned in Chapter 12. And, we have learned that the Oregon Supreme Court refused to enforce the applicable law which is of itself a criminal act. Also, we have learned that the people have no criminal prosecutorial powers but are subject to whatever the government decides.

Appendices Y thru Y-3 show the current appeal before the Board of Property Tax Appeals – 2009-2010 PERSONAL PROPERTY PETITION.

Please, pray that GOD will reward the righteous and punish the wickedly recalcitrant public servants.

AND, we should never forget that we have the freedom to exercise our 1st Amendment and other rights; because, we are protected by our volunteer military, police and other security forces.

All of America is deeply indebted to you ! THANK YOU ! !

APPENDICES

Understanding Corruption in Oregon

PROPERTY DESCRIPTION   YAMHILL COUNTY, OREGON   ACCOUNT NO: 508939
01156 SW WESTVALE ST   535 NE FIFTH STREET
MCMINNVILLE   MCMINNVILLE, OR 97128
                                 (503) 434-7521 (HOURS: 8:30 AM-5:00 PM M-F)

LAST YEAR'S TAX $920.18

See back for explanation of taxes marked with (‡)

PIN #: M00239797   CHEMEKETA COMM COLL   34.45
CODE: 40.0 PCA: 0195   MCMINNVILLE SD 40   228.37
                           YAMHILL ESD   19.90

                           EDUCATION TOTAL: 282.72

GALL JOSEPH &
GALL DARLENE M   MH P P A   6.00
1156 SW WESTVALE ST   CHEMEKETA LIBRARY   4.50
MCMINNVILLE OR 97128   MCMINNVILLE   276.28
                           YAM CO SOIL & WATER   1.95
                           YAMHILL CO EXT SERV   2.47
VALUES: LAST YEAR THIS YEAR   YAMHILL COUNTY   141.54
REAL MARKET-RMV

                                   GENERAL GOVT TOTAL: 432.76
  STRUCTURES: 69,742   59,281
TOTAL RMV: 69,742   59,281   CHEMEKETA COMM COLL   7.45
                                   MCMINNVILLE   69.64
ASSESSED: 53,433   55,036   MCMINNVILLE SD 40   164.98
  EXEMPTION:
                                   BONDS - OTHER TOTAL: 242.07

NET TAXABLE: 53,433   55,036   TOTAL 2002-03 TAXES: 957.53
1995 MARLETTE 27X60

          +.9708 %

If a mortgage company pays your taxes,
This statement is for your records only.

Full Payment with 3% Discount	2/3 Payment with 2% Discount	1/3 Payment No Discount	TOTAL TAX (After Discount)
$928.81	$625.59	$319.18	$928.81

A

YAMHILL COUNTY
PROPERTY TAX RECEIPT FISCAL YEAR: 2002
(503)434-7521

PIN#: M00239797   AMOUNT PAID: 928.81 001 ACCOUNT#: 508939
RECEIPT NUMBER: 2716   RECEIPT DATE: 11/04/2002

PAID BY: GALL JOSEPH & DARLENE
YEAR	LEVIED TAX	TAX PAID	FEE PAID	16% INT	12%INT/DISC	UNPAID TA
2002 1	957.53+	957.53-			28.72-	
2001 1	920.18+					
2000 1	885.77+					
1999 1	878.00+					
1998 1	846.24+					
0						
0						

***** UNPAID TAX DOES NOT INCLUDE ACCRUING INTEREST *****
BALANCES AND AMOUNTS PAID INCLUDE CORRECTIONS TO DATE
SITUS: 1156 SW WESTVALE ST
197   MCMINNVILLE

GALL JOSEPH &
GALL DARLENE M
1156 SW WESTVALE ST   CODES: 40.0
MCMINNVILLE OR 97128   DONE: Y0

A-1

YAMHILL COUNTY PROGRAM & FUNCTIONAL ORGANIZATION

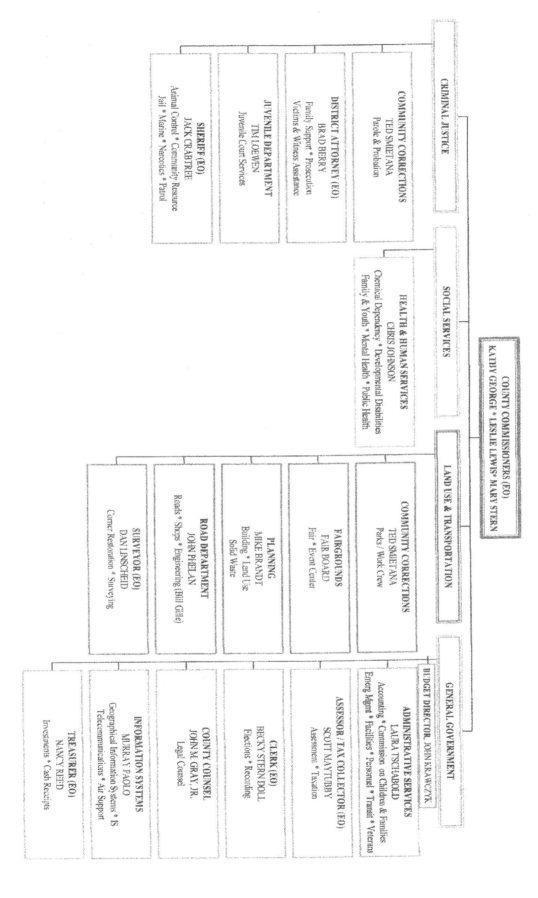

COUNTY COMMISSIONERS (EO)
KATHY GEORGE * LESLIE LEWIS * MARY STERN

CRIMINAL JUSTICE

COMMUNITY CORRECTIONS
TED SMIETANA
Parole & Probation

DISTRICT ATTORNEY (EO)
BRAD BERRY
Family Support * Prosecution
Victims & Witness Assistance

JUVENILE DEPARTMENT
TIM LOEWEN
Juvenile Court Services

SHERIFF (EO)
JACK CRABTREE
Animal Control * Community Resource
Jail * Marine * Narcotics * Patrol

SOCIAL SERVICES

HEALTH & HUMAN SERVICES
CHRIS JOHNSON
Chemical Dependency * Developmental Disabilities
Family & Youth * Mental Health * Public Health

LAND USE & TRANSPORTATION

COMMUNITY CORRECTIONS
TED SMIETANA
Parks / Work Crew

FAIRGROUNDS
FAIR BOARD
Fair * Event Center

PLANNING
MIKE BRANDT
Building * Land Use
Solid Waste

ROAD DEPARTMENT
JOHN PHELAN
Roads * Shops * Engineering (Bill Gille)

SURVEYOR (EO)
DAN LINSCHEID
Corner Restoration * Surveying

GENERAL GOVERNMENT

BUDGET DIRECTOR, JOHN KRAWCZYK

ADMINISTRATIVE SERVICES
LAURA TSCHABOLD
Accounting * Commission on Children & Families
Emerg Mgmt * Facilities * Personnel * Transit * Veterans

ASSESSOR / TAX COLLECTOR (EO)
SCOTT MAYTUBBY
Assessment * Taxation

CLERK (EO)
BECKY STERN DOLL
Elections * Recording

COUNTY COUNSEL
JOHN M. GRAY, JR.
Legal Counsel

INFORMATION SYSTEMS
MURRAY PAOLO
Geographical Information Systems * IS
Telecommunications * Air Support

TREASURER (EO)
NANCY REED
Investments * Cash Receipts

BEFORE THE YAMHILL COUNTY BOARD OF PROPERTY TAX APPEALS

Real Property
Stipulated Agreement

In the Matter of the Petition of
Joseph & Darlene Gall
1156 SW Westvale St
McMinnville, Oregon 97128

Petitioner's Name and Address

Petition No. _____ 34 134.1

Account No. _____ 508939

Tax year _____ 2002

The above-named petitioner and the assessor of Yamhill County have entered into the following agreement concerning the valuation of the above-described property.

Real Market Value (RMV)

	From	To
Land	$0	$0
Structures, etc.	$0	$0
MS	$59,281	$43,000
Total	$59,281	$43,000

RMV of Exception

	From	To
Land	$0	$0
Structures, etc.	$0	$0
MS	$0	$0
Total	$0	$0

Maximum Assessed Value

	From	To
Total	$55,036	$55,036

Assessed Value

	From	To
Total	$43,000	$43,000

The parties to this appeal agree to the correction of values as indicated above and request the board of property tax appeals issue an order reflecting this change.

		Susan DeBolt
Petitioner or Representative (print or type)	Petitioner or Representative (print or type)	County Officer (print or type)
		Appraiser
Title (if applicabe)	Title (if applicabe)	Title
		Susan DeBolt
Signature of Petitioner or Representative	Signature of Petitioner or Representative	Signature of County Officer
		1-14-03
Date	Date	Date

Please indicate whether you wish to attend the hearing: Yes _____   No _____

Reason: Owner paid $43,000 11/01.

Reviewed by _M. Jough_   Date: 1/14/03

C

Charles Stern
Yamhill County Clerk
535 NE. 5th, McMinnville, OR 97128-4593 Ph. 503.434.7518 Fax 503.434.7520
Email: sternc@co.yamhill.or.us

Petition No. 34 4 34. 1

Dear Board of Property Tax Appeals Petitioner,

Enclosed you will find a stipulation agreement form for your consideration. After examining your petition to the Board of Property Tax Appeals, the assessor has agreed that your property should be valued as stated on the enclosed form. Please examine the values and, if you agree to the values as stipulated, sign and return one copy of the stipulation agreement in the postage paid envelope. The second copy of the stipulation agreement is for your records.

YOUR IMMEDIATE REPLY to this letter is requested. If your acceptance of the stipulation is received no later than Monday, February 3, the assessor can correct the values as stipulated. A hearing will be held, and unless you wish to do so, it will not be necessary for you to attend. If you do not agree with the values as stipulated, mark the box below on this form and return this letter with your unsigned stipulation agreement; a hearing for your petition will then be scheduled.

If you do not agree to this stipulation, your quick response to this notice will be appreciated so that hearings can be scheduled immediately after the session convenes on February 3rd.

☑   Check this box if you do not agree with the stipulation agreement and return this letter with the unsigned stipulation agreement.

If you need assistance in this matter, please do not hesitate to call Jan or Marsha at 503-434-7518.

Marsha Gabriel
Clerk
Board of Property Tax Appeals

C-1

ASSESSOR'S OFFICE

M00239797

40.0

GALL JOSEPH &
GALL DARLENE M
1156 SW WESTVALE ST
MCMINNVILLE   OR 97128

Is the above address correct? If not please change here so we may update our records.

Explanation of Sales Questionnaire

Why is this information needed?

Real Estate Sales are used as one factor in determining Assessed Value for Taxation. Sales are also used
to measure uniformity of Real Market Values. The use of these sales has been tested in the courts.

How will this information be used?

Trained appraisers will consider the selling price of your property and the selling price of similar properties to
determine the Real Market Value for many properties. Present day building construction costs, age of the
buildings, location, etc., will also be considered.

Why are so many questions asked about my property?

Many things can affect the selling price of Manufactured Structures. Was it a cash transaction, an estate,
or were special deals for financing given. Many times the sale of a Manufactured Structure will be included in a
land sale, it is very helpful if we can determine the price for the Manufactured Structure alone. The sale
price may also include items such as furniture, equipment, or appliances not built in, if so please list these
items and the value, so we may correctly compare the Real Market Value with the Sale Price.

Will my taxes be raised if I answer this questionnaire?

Not because you answer these questions. Property tax increases are caused by increasing costs of operating
schools, cities, water districts, and the many other public services supported by property taxes. From the
passage of Measure 50, most tax assessments will only raise 3% each year, unless a major change has
been made to the property. Accurate sale information makes possible accurate Real Market Values.

What other items should be noted?

Delinquent taxes, special assessments or other expenses that are part of the sale price should be noted. Any
changes made to the property should be noted so our Real Market Value can be properly compared to the sale
price. Any address changes can be made on this form and we will be sure to change them. This is important
even if your mortgage company pays your taxes, you will receive a copy also, but only if we have the right
mailing address.

Please fill out the back side of this questionnaire, sign and date the form, then return in pre-paid envelope.

If you have any questions concerning this form, please call our Data Analyst at (503)434-7521.

THANK YOU

PRINTED: 09/30/2002
PIN #: M00239797
PCA: 0195   STAT CLASS: 467
SITUS: 1156 SW WESTVALE ST
MCMINNVILLE

ACCOUNT #: 508939
NEIGHBORHOOD: KAT5
SPACE #: 19700

REVIEW:
   B OF E:
   D OF R:

OWNER: GALL JOSEPH &
AGENT:
           CONSIDERATION: $43,000   REJECTION CODE: 33
VIN: HO11526AB   TITLE DATE: 01/02/2002
MAKE: MARLETTE   SALE DATE: 12/13/2001
RP PIN#: R4430AB 00100   MODEL:

LEVY CODE: 40.0   CLASS: 06   YEAR BUILT: 1995
CONSTR GRP: 02   SIZE: 27X60   BEDRMS/BATHS: 02 / 2.0
INT INSP/LVL: Y 0   QUALITY: 0.05   APPR DATE: 07/19
APPRAISER: DB   TABLE ID: 1992   RP ADDITION: N

***** STRUCTURAL COMPONENTS *****

DESCRIPTION	CLASS	UNITS	OTHER
FOUND - POST & PIER		0	
EXT COV - MASONITE		0	
ROOF - GABLE		0	
ROOFCOV - COMP SHINGLE		0	
FLOORCOV - CARPET COMBO		0	
INTCOV - DRYWALL		0	
H & C - FORCED AIR		0	
KITCABS - HARDWOOD		0	
COUNTERS - PLASTICS		0	
EAVES	06	0	
GUTTERS	06	120	
DOWNSPOUTS	06	0	

***** COMPUTATIONS (MFD STRUCTURE) *****

CLASS	SQ FT	X	BC/SQFT	+	BC/LUMP SUM	X	LCM	=	COST NEW
06	1620		18.04		6288		0.18		41905

***** BUILDING ADJUSTMENTS *****

DESCRIPTION	UNITS	X	COST	X	LCM	=	COST NEW
GUTTERS	120		2.00		0.18		283
KIT APPL - DISHWASHER	1		0.00		0.00		0
KIT APPL - COOKTOP	1		0.00		0.00		0
KIT APPL - SGL OVEN	1		0.00		0.00		0
KIT APPL - HOOD & FAN	1		0.00		0.00		0
PLUMB - SHOWER/GLASS/ENC	1		0.00		0.00		0
SKIRT - WOOD	174		6.55		0.18		1345
PLUMB - GARDEN TUB/FBG	1		0.00		0.00		0

COST NEW	X	QUALITY(%)	X	DEPR (%)	=	DEPR REPL COST
43533		0.05		1.00		45710

E

Appeal of Property Value

	Real Market Value (RMV) from tax statement or assessor's records	Real Market Value (RMV) requested by petitioner
27 Land	$	$
28 Buildings, machinery, etc.	$	$
29 Manufactured structure	$ 59,281	$ 43,000
30 Total RMV	$ 59,281	$ 43,000
31 Total assessed value (AV) from tax statement or assessor's records	→ $ 55,036	

Basis of Appeal (attach additional pages if necessary)

32 The purchase price approximates the real market value; however, the declining market suggest the RMV is less or it should be less than the purshase price

Evidence of Real Market Value of Property

...stings, appraisals (attach complete report), construction bids, e

☒ Yes ☐ No If yes, complete the following:

NEWS-REGISTER/McMINNVILLE, OREGON

Purchase Price: 43,000

☐ Yes ☒ No Name of real estate office: _____

...e years? ☐ Yes ☒ No If yes, complete the following:

...anufactured Homes

NEW Triple-Wide
...ncludes fireplace. 50" TV
...and Kit., 4 bdrm. $64,995.
...CADE HOMES 800-485-8175

...ove in Now, Many Extras
...rm, 2 Ba $650.00 per month oac
...New carpet, fresh paint, tile,
...armon Homes 503-318-1787

133 Manufactured Homes

Why would anyone buy a factory-built housing unit when Adair Homes will build a real home for about the same price? Call Adair (503)645-3547

NEWBERG...

Dates offered for sale: _____

☐ No Name of real estate office: _____

...? ☐ Yes ☐ No If yes, complete the following:

Date of appraisal: _____

Name of appraiser: _____

...three years? ☐ Yes ☒ No If yes, complete the follow

Changes made: _____

Dates of construction: _____   Cost of new construction: _____

Declaration:
I declare under the penalties for false swearing [ORS 305.990(4)] that I have examined this document, and to the be knowledge, it is true, correct, and complete.

37 Signature and name of petitioner or petitioner's representative (attach authorization if necessary)   DARLENE M. GALL   38 Date

X _Joseph Gall_ _Darlene M. Gall_ Print or type name _Joseph Gall_   12/30

Sign name

When and Where to File your Petition

Appeal petitions must be filed with the board of property tax appeals by **December 31, 2002.** File your petition with the county clerk in the county where the property is located. Mail or deliver your petition to the address shown in the box. →

Please return this petition to:

CHARLES STERN, CO. CLERK
YAMHILL COUNTY
535 E. 5TH ST.
McMINNVILLE, OR 97128-4593
503-434-7518
FAX 434-7520

F

IN THE SUPREME COURT
of the STATE OF OREGON

Joseph Gall, pro se
    Plaintiff - Appellant,

       V

Department of Revenue
State of Oregon
    Defendant(s) - Respondent
      et al

Tax Court Case No. 4767

S054580

APPELLANT's — MOTION — Reconsider Order

To revisit and to issue a DECISION — to move beyond this court's ORDER HOLDING
PETITION FOR RECONSIDERATION IN ABEYANCE, dated
November 21, **2007.**

1.

Appeal from the judgment of the Tax Court for Yamhill County, Honorable

Henry C. Breithaupt, Judge.

<u>Appellant, pro se</u>

Joseph Gall

1156 SW Westvale St

McMinnville, OR 97128

Phone: 503-472-1502

<u>Attorney for Respondent</u>

Douglas M. Adair #95195

Assistant Attorney General

Department of Justice

1162 Court Street NE

Salem, OR 97301-4096

Phone: 503-947-4530

G

2.

This MOTION is warranted because - the 2008-2009 Tax Statement received from the Yamhill County tax assessor is clear evidence that the Oregon Department of Revenue (DOR) **does not** intend to comply with existing law - State and Federal.

This court has an obligation to rule, without delay, in accordance with the facts and applicable law(JR 2-107).

3.

RELIEF SOUGHT -- as stated in :

1. TC-MD 060207C / TC 4767 COMPLAINT (s) ; and,

2. SC-S054580 Plaintiff-Appellant BRIEF ; also,

3. Requesting this court to reinstate the creditability -- the honorable intent of Plaintiff-Appellant -- within this state and on the world-wide internet. Court assertions that Plaintiff-Appellant has filed frivolous appeals is ludicrous -- without merit !

4.

FACTS

1:   Plaintiff/Appellant has received from the Yamhill County assessor (David Lawson) his 2008-2009 tax assessment upon my *personal property*.(Encl: #1)

This assessment is **without** legal authority ; also, the assessed value increase of 9 % **violates** the 3 % limitation set by ORS 308.146 :

308.146 Determination of maximum assessed value and assessed value; reduction in maximum assessed value following property destruction; effect of

conservation or highway scenic preservation easement. (1) The maximum assessed value of property shall equal 103 percent of the property's assessed value from the prior year or 100 percent of the property's maximum assessed value from the prior year, whichever is greater.

A similar increase was challenged in TC-MD 060207C ; and, in TC 4767 COMPLAINT , paragraph 10. on page 6. - other increases were cited as high as 67 %.

This assessor , with impunity , has *knowingly and willfully* <u>ignored</u> Oregon law for *personal gain* (ORS 162.415) – the collected taxes support his salary and the Oregon retirement system.

2:   The assessment form states "Personal property can be seized and other financial assets can be garnished."

3:   This is EXTORTION UNDER COLOR OF OFFICIAL RIGHT = TYRANNY

4:   The language in " ORS 164.075 Theft by extortion ." - identifies the conditions of this very egregious malfeasance and nonfeasance perpetrated upon Plaintiff/Appellant and other mobile home owners in Yamhill County and in the entire State of Oregon.

5:   DOR , the Tax Court and this Court have acknowledged that this property is sited on rented land not owned by Plaintiff/Appellant (ORS 308.875).

6:   Hardy Meyers - Oregon Attorney General - has **<u>not</u>** prosecuted anyone.

7:   Governor Kulongoski has **<u>not enforced</u>** the law although requested to do so.

 # 8: The Commission on Judicial Fitness and Disability said " Your request is is denied".

 # 9: The Oregon State Bar responded with – " Your concerns do not fall within the bar's jurisdiction".

 # 10: Plaintiff/Appellant's first appeal was filed with the Board of Property Tax Appeals(BOPTA) in December **2002** and every subsequent year ; and, did file another appeal before the deadline of December 31, 2008 (Encl: # 2).

 # 11: DOR **mis**represented mobile home/manufactured homes as a Measure 50 **real** *property classification.*

 # 12: During the first Tax Court trial(TC 4639) , Plaintiff submitted into evidence copies of ORS 308.875 that clearly classifies , more than 65,000 , Oregon mobile homes as **personal property.**

 # 13: Tax Court Magistrates in TC-MD030131B and TC-MD060207C **mis**represented the law by *ignoring* phrases such as - "Except as otherwise specifically provided"(ORS 308.105) , and "except as otherwise provided by law"(ORS 307.030).

 # 14: Tax Court Judge Henry C. Breithaupt defied his oath - twice - to rule for DOR in TC 4639 and TC 4675.

 # 15: Justice W. Michael Gillette in SC-S51473 and Justice Rives Kistler in SC-S054580 - defied their oath to rule *contrary* to the facts and applicable law.

G

16: Plaintiff/Appellant's BRIEF APPENDICES(S054580) cited many, but not all, laws applicable to the taxation of manufactured homes sited in Mobile Home Parks throughout the State of Oregon.

17: Plaintiff/Appellant's BRIEF(S054580) on page 3. states that **"Value is not the question:** The ad valorem taxation of this personal property violates FEDERAL and State law. Taxation of this *personal* property under COLOR OF OFFICIAL RIGHT is extortion, theft and violates other laws which is : criminal conduct ".

18: Oregon law does not assess ad valorem tax on 'personal' property such as : household possessions, cars, motor homes, boats, yachts etc. Many of these items have a real market value much higher than the average manufactured home.

19: Arizona recognizes HUD's classification of manufactured homes as 'personal' property - Arizona treats them as they do cars etc.

20: Oregon's split classification of manufactured homes in ORS 308.875 is, without doubt, a *deceitful* challenge to HUD's classification to generate funds for State redistribution . This is most definitely **un**constitutional. Gibbons v Ogden in 1824 upheld THE CONSTITUTION OF THE UNITED STATES, Article IV.

21: Many public officers are acting in "an organized resistance to established government" - INSURRECTION. These public officers must be prosecuted and banned from public service in accordance with the BILL OF RIGHTS, Article XIV, Section 3.

22:   Oregon law(ORS 162.415) says a public servant is required to be inherently competent within the office.

23:   Oregon law(ORS 162.235) prohibits "Obstructing governmental or judicial administration". This is addressed in the Oregon Code of Professional Conduct, Rule 8.3 and 8.4(4).

24:   Plaintiff/Appellant has petitioned the Yamhill County Sheriff to arrest and the Yamhill County District Attorney to prosecute these known violators; however, the pleas have fallen on deaf ears.

25:   Allegations have been written by the Oregon Tax Courts and sustained by this Court in its OPINION(S054580) . These allegations were egregious *dishonesty* to charge Plaintiff/Appellant with frivolous appeals. This Court has an opportunity, when it writes its DECISION, to hold accountable the judges responsible for their *bad Behaviour*.

26:   This manufactured home owner does not have the monies to hire a lawyer to challenge the *illegal* actions of DOR and other Oregon public officers .

27:   Sir Walter Scott, a Scottish author and novelist wrote – Oh what a tangled web we weave, When first we practice to deceive !

　　　　This describes, very well, the trail of court opinions and decisions associated with Plaintiff/Appellant' petitions.

G

28: The Holy Bible gives us good advice -

Thou shalt not steal.

Thou shalt not bear false witness.

Thou shalt not covet.

29: The Holy Bible - Romans 13:1 - Everyone must submit to governing authorities. For all authority comes from God, and those in positions of authority have been placed there by God.

These words were written by Apostle Paul, he goes on to say in 13:5 So you must submit to them, not only to avoid punishment, but also to keep a clear conscience.

30: Plaintiff/Appellant does not object to *legal* taxation; however, **illegal** taxation is challenged because it is an abomination committed upon the citizenry.

31: In the criminal law, a conspiracy is an agreement between natural persons to break the law at some time in the future, and, in some cases, with at least one overt act in furtherance of that agreement. ... en.wikipedia.org/wiki/Conspiracy_(crime)

32: **DEFENSE, WITHDRAWAL FROM CONSPIRACY - A conspiracy does not become a crime until two things have occurred: First, the making of the agreement, and; Second, the performance of some overt act by one of the conspirators.**

So, if a person enters into a conspiracy agreement but later changes his mind and withdraws from that agreement before anyone has committed an overt act, then the

G

crime was not complete at that time and the person who withdrew cannot be convicted, he would be not guilty of the alleged conspiracy offense.

However, in order to decide that a person withdrew from a conspiracy the person he must have taken affirmative action to disavow or defeat the purpose of the conspiracy; and, as just explained, he must have taken such action before he or any other member of the scheme had committed any overt act.

33: AIDING AND ABETTING (AGENCY) - The guilt of a person in a criminal case may be proved without evidence that he personally did every act involved in the commission of the crime charged. The law recognizes that, ordinarily, anything a person can do for himself may also be accomplished through direction of another person as an agent, or by acting together with, or under the direction of, another person or persons in a joint effort.

So, if the acts or conduct of an agent, employee or other associate of the person are willfully directed or authorized by the person, or if the person aids and abets another person by willfully joining together with that person in the commission of a crime, then the law holds the person responsible for the conduct of that other person just as though the person had engaged in such conduct himself.x Notice, however, that before any person can be held criminally responsible for the conduct of others it is necessary that the person willfully associate himself in some way with the crime, and willfully participate in it. Mere presence at the scene of a crime and even knowledge that a crime is being committed are not sufficient to establish that a person either directed or aided and abetted the crime.

#34:   The recent loss of billions of dollars in the Oregon retirement funds – reported by the press - doesn't justify violations of law in areas of Oregon government.!

#35:   DOR's "How To Appeal Your Property Value" (Encl:#3) contains

misrepresentations of Measure 50 (codified into the Oregon Constitution).

   This is pertinent because DOR has taxed Plaintiff-Appellant's *personal* property as if it is *real* property.

   "Incompetency or malfeasance of public officer" may be tried as criminal offenses.

Because the misrepresentations are associated with a tax assessment -- this must be prosecuted as a Class B Felony(ORS 164.075).

Applicable law

Plaintiff/Appellant's BRIEF APPENDICES(S054580) itemizes many laws applicable to this case: but, the list is not complete. This Court, with its access to the brightest minds coming out of the Oregon law schools, should have no problems researching all applicable law governing the conduct of public officers and their duties.

Although many laws apply to this case we need to look at only **four(4) statutes** to decide this case *rationally and objectively* with respect to the ad valorem tax applicable to manufactured homes *classified as personal property*.

ORS 308.875 - "If the manufactured structure is owned separately and apart from the land upon which it is located, it shall be assessed and taxed as personal property." . . . "Manufactured structures need not be returned under ORS 308.290."

ORS 308.290(2)(a) "Each return of personal property shall contain a full listing of such property and a statement of its real market value," . . .

These two statutes establish classification and the reporting of value ; however, since a return stating a real market value is **waived** in ORS 308.875 - there cannot be an assessment on a '0' base except for the following statute.

G

ORS 446.525 Special assessment; collection. (1) A special assessment is levied annually upon each manufactured dwelling that is assessed for ad valorem property tax purposes as personal property. The amount of the assessment is $6.

ORS 307.032(2) Unless determined under a provision of law governing the special assessment, ...

The first of these two laws establish a special assessment for a manufactured dwelling(home) classified as *personal* property and the amount assessed. The second statute **waives** the usual value and assessment requirements for personal property.

5.

It is **abundantly clear** that the Oregon LEGISLATURE intended to adhere to *HUD's classification* for manufactured homes as **personal property** . The exemption for personal property as stated in ORS 307.190 does not include these homes ; consequently, the LEGISLATURE provided law - to recognize their constitutional duty as within the four statutes cited in paragraph 4. above.

6.

Also, it is **abundantly clear** that Elizabeth Harchenko, Director of the Department of Revenue will not voluntarily comply with the aforementioned Oregon law cited in paragraph 4. above - she has so stated in a communiqué **mis**representing other Oregon law as authorizing authority.

7.

Plaintiff-Appellant requests this court order Defendant-Respondent to state their perceived authority to assess ad valorem taxes upon manufactured homes classified as *personal property*.

8.

The Oregon LEGISLATURE has given the Oregon Supreme Court - **Chief Justice** broad *authorities and responsibilities*. It is time for a clean sweep. Time to take decisive action. Time to disbar, remove and prosecute the following who have chosen to participate in a *corrupt conspiracy* to ignore Oregon law : Justice Gillette; Justice Kistler Tax Court Judges – Breithaupt, Robinson, Mattson ; Governor Kulongoski ; Attorney General Hardy Meyers ; Solicitor General Mary H. William ; DOR Director Elizabeth Harchenko ; DOR Attorney Douglas M. Adair ; DOR Attorney James C. Wallace Yamhill County – District Attorney Bradley C. Berry, attorneys Gray and Sanai ; Washington County attorney Fun ; the complicit Judges and attorneys - at the Commission on Judicial Fitness and Disability , at the Oregon State Bar ; and the law clerks who participated in writing the Opinions and Decisions for the Courts.

The people of Oregon experienced something similar in 1910 causing a referendum to pass - codified within the Oregon Consitution :   .

G

Oregon CONSTITUTION , Article VII

Section 6. Incompetency or malfeasance of public officer. Public officers shall not be impeached; but incompetency, corruption, malfeasance or delinquency in office may be tried in the same manner as criminal offenses, and judgment may be given of dismissal from office, and such further punishment as may have been prescribed by law. [Created through initiative petition filed July 7, 1910, and adopted by the people Nov. 8, 1910]

There can be no doubt that the people want their government to be honest and that they demand *prosecution in accordance with the law.*

9.

No — it isn't **bravery** to make revealing statements as in the foregoing paragraphs within this MOTION and the preceding petitions for justice.

However, those who signed the Declaration of Independence showed great courage defying the oppressive power of the British Crown.

Also, General Washington's army and every army throughout American history have fought bravely for and in defense of our freedom.

A patriot will not, must not acquiesce to the subversive forces who are attempting to establish an oligarchy within the Executive and Judicial branches of Oregon government.

January 07, 2009

Joseph Gall
1156 SW Westvale St
McMinnville, OR 97128

G

IN THE SUPREME COURT OF THE STATE OF OREGON

JOSEPH GALL,
Plaintiff-Appellant,

v.

DEPARTMENT OF REVENUE,
Defendant-Respondent.

Oregon Tax Court No. 4767

Oregon Supreme Court No. S054580

ORDER HOLDING PETITION FOR RECONSIDERATION IN ABEYANCE

Upon consideration by the court.

The Supreme Court has decided that it should withhold final action on the petition for reconsideration until the court has decided *Department of Revenue v. Croslin*, 19 OTR 69 (2006) (S054012). The court heard oral arguments in that case on September 6, 2007, and it is under advisement.

It is so ordered that the petition for reconsideration shall remain pending in the Supreme Court until further order of the court.

_____November 21, 2007_____
DATE

_____
CHIEF JUSTICE

c: Joseph Gall
   Douglas M Adair

jk

H

DEPARTMENT OF JUSTICE
GENERAL COUNSEL DIVISION

January 8, 2009

Graciela Rivera
Judicial Department
1163 State Street
Salem, OR 97301-2563

Re: *Joseph Gall v. Department of Revenue*
Supreme Court Case No. S054580
Tax Court Case No. 4767
DOJ File No. 150303-GT0137-07

Dear Ms. Rivera:

Defendant, Department of Revenue, will not file a response to Appellant's MOTION – Reconsideration Order filed on or about January 7, 2009. Plaintiff's motion merely repeats or restates frivolous and groundless arguments that do not merit further response.

Sincerely,

Douglas M. Adair
Senior Assistant Attorney General
Tax & Finance Section

JUSTICE-#1241702-v1
c: Joseph Gall

JOSEPH GALL,
Plaintiff-Appellant,

v.

DEPARTMENT OF REVENUE,
Defendant-Respondent.

Tax Court
4767

S054580

ORDER DENYING PETITION FOR RECONSIDERATION AND DISMISSING AS MOOT MOTION TO RECONSIDER ORDER HOLDING IN ABEYANCE

Upon consideration by the court.

The court has considered the petition for reconsideration and orders that it be denied.

Appellant's motion to reconsider order holding in abeyance is dismissed as moot.

February 11, 2009
DATE

CHIEF JUSTICE

c: Joseph Gall
Douglas M Adair

gar/S054580odrc090211

ORDER DENYING PETITION FOR RECONSIDERATION AND DISMISSING AS MOOT MOTION TO RECONSIDER ORDER HOLDING IN ABEYANCE

J

Joseph Gall, pro se
    Plaintiff - Appellant,

        V

Department of Revenue
State of Oregon
    Defendant(s) - Respondent
        et al

Tax Court Case No. 4767

S054580

MOTION to waive rules
for *good cause* and to
review En Banc

<u>1.</u>

<u>Appellant, pro se</u>

Joseph Gall

1156 SW Westvale St

McMinnville, OR 97128

Phone: 503-472-1502

<u>Attorney for Respondent</u>

Douglas M. Adair #95195

Assistant Attorney General

Department of Justice

1162 Court Street NE

Salem, OR 97301-4096

Phone: 503-947-4530

2.

With authority of the OREGON RULES OF APPELLATE PROCEDURES –

ORAP Rule 1.20 (5) – Plaintiff / Appellant petitions this court, in the interest of justice,

to waive whatever rules necessary to review, to reconsider this court's decisions.

K

3.

RELIEF SOUGHT

Plaintiff / Appellant submits this plea to set aside the tax court DECISIONS and previous DECISIONS / ORDERS of this court.

This plea requests this court to re-instate Plaintiff / Appellant *reputation* that has been denigrated by the publishing of court decisions - court decisions that *misrepresent* established law.

Plaintiff / Appellant requests this court to award monies as stated in the BRIEF – and, refund the tax court ordered (May 11, 2009) costs and attorney fees that were not awarded by this court in its DECISION. Furthermore, Respondent did not file a timely claim in accordance with ORS 20.320.

Additionally, *sanction*, as this court sees fit in its wisdom, the recalcitrant public officers who have ***knowingly and willfully*** submitted false statements and claims before this court; e.g. in the RESPONDENTS' BRIEF.

4.

Plaintiff / Appellant was not aware, until recently, of certain law applicable to this case before this court. This case has embedded in the record many violations of law perpetrated by a number of public officers – serious violations that we cannot ignore or mitigate.

5.

I am an old man, born December 24, 1930, with one foot toward spiritual eternity, who can remember when the oath was said with a duty before GOD, who can remember when the law was not misrepresented by our public officers to support an agenda, when honesty was a treasured character trait, when a handshake was a binding contract, when the law was enforced, when we had a trust in government to protect a citizen regardless of education or social status, when public service was considered an honorable profession, when military service was recognized with accolades, when marriage meant one man and one woman, when the government displayed with pride reference to GOD our creator, when the sanctity of life was supported by government. YES, I am an old man petitioning my State government for *redress of grievances*.

6.

Department of Revenue(DOR) attorney Douglas M. Adair misrepresented certain tax law by injecting the word – *additional*. The tax court accepted this as a legitimate legal argument and this court affirmed the tax court decision.

However, this court, Justice Balmer disagrees with the tax court position –

In the Oregon Supreme Court : Justice Balmer writes -
Garrison v Department of Revenue , TC 4796 ; SC S055852 ; Dec 31, 2008
    We agree that a judicial or agency rule that conflicts with a statute is invalid to the extent that it so conflicts and that a rule created within a statutory scheme cannot amend, alter, enlarge upon, or limit statutory wording so that it has the effect of undermining the legislative intent. *See Miller v. Employment Division*, 290 Or 285, 289, 620 P2d 1377 (1980) ("An agency may not amend, alter, enlarge or limit the terms of a legislative enactment by rule.").

Additionally –

"An unconstitutional act is not law; it confers no rights; it imposes no duties; affords no protection; it creates no office; it is in legal contemplation, as inoperative as though it had never been passed." Norton vs. Shelby County 118 US 425 p. 442.

3

K

As I read and re-read the record of MOTIONS and DECISIONS – and then read the tax court trial transcript and listen to the tax court trial audio it is abundantly clear that tax court Judge Breithaupt has a deeply engrained disdain for a citizen who has the audacity to navigate through the jungle of court rules to file a petition for oneself – he believes that only a judge or lawyer has the intellect to read and understand the law forgetting the Constitution of Oregon mandates simple language -

ARTICLE IV

LEGISLATIVE DEPARTMENT

Section 21. Acts to be plainly worded. Every act, and joint resolution shall be plainly worded, avoiding as far as practicable the use of technical terms.–

As you read the tax court trial transcript and listen to the trial audio – you will witness a judge who is angry – that a common citizen has uncovered and challenged a *fraudulent scheme to steal* from some of the poorest citizens of this State.

Consequently, tax court Judge Breithaupt resorted to *abusive intimidation* throughout the pre-trial telephone conferences and during the trial; e.g. in the transcript of TC 4767 on page 61 lines 22-25 and on page 62 lines 1-3 he says – ". . . because I don't want to see you and your wife hurt again. If you choose to read documents that demonstrate your victory and if you choose to read them as part of a conspiracy it's gonna be a trouble for you. It's gonna be trouble for you. If you choose to accuse the state and the county of being dishonest and relying on repealed statutes when in fact they haven't, it's gonna be trouble for you."

The quote sounds like a direct *threat* ! Obviously this shows that Judge Breithaupt had already decided to *wrongfully* use ORS 305.437 to *intimidate* , to *deter* another petition for redress - it worked against me and the imposition of a $5,000.00 fine followed by his order to pay the cost and attorney fees reinforced his anger. No other petition has been filed(to best of my knowledge)on this issue. But he acknowledges that questions of honesty were raised by this petitioner.

Then the tax court splashed across the internet their brazen disregard for the truth and the law – their DECISIONS. Without doubt this was intended to destroy my *reputation* and creditability - violations of :

OREGON CONSTITUTION

ARTICLE I

BILL OF RIGHTS

Section 10. Administration of justice. No court shall be secret, but justice shall be administered, openly and without purchase, completely and without delay, and every man **shall have remedy by due course of law for injury done him** in **his person, property, or reputation.–**

Without doubt these *intimidation* tactics are , also, violations of –

ORS 162.235 Obstructing governmental or judicial administration. (1) A person commits the crime of obstructing governmental or judicial administration if the person intentionally obstructs, impairs or hinders the administration of law or other governmental or judicial function **by means of intimidation, force, physical or economic interference or obstacle.**

(2) This section shall not apply to the obstruction of unlawful governmental or judicial action or interference with the making of an arrest.

(3) Obstructing governmental or judicial administration is a Class A misdemeanor. [1971 c.743 §198; 1981 c.902 §1]

K

ARTICLE I

BILL OF RIGHTS

Section 16. Excessive bail and fines; cruel and unusual punishments; power of jury in criminal case. Excessive bail shall not be required, <u>nor excessive fines imposed</u>. Cruel and unusual punishments shall not be inflicted, but all penalties shall be proportioned to the offense.–

In all criminal cases whatever, the jury shall have the right to determine the law, and the facts under the direction of the Court as to the law, <u>**and the right of new trial, as in civil cases.**</u>

The intimidation tactics have worked for the tax court - court case reduction from 2000(78 cases) to 2007(26 cases) - a reduction of nearly 70 % reported by the OREGON BLUE BOOK : http://bluebook.state.or.us/state/judicial/judicial28.htm

Should this be *condoned* by the Chief Justice of this Supreme Court who has the authority to sanction any judge who violates his oath of office? <u>**Absolutely not**</u> ! What sanctions should be imposed on the *three* tax court judges? The answer is in The BILL OF RIGHTS, Article XIV, Section 3.

8..

To repeat anything already in the record would be redundant but perhaps I have already done so – I've tried not to. This MOTION is submitted in good faith to test the *veracity* of Oregon's justice system.

August 2009

Respectfully submitted,

Joseph Gall

Joseph Gall

IN THE SUPREME COURT OF THE STATE OF OREGON

Date: August 12, 2009

To: Joseph Gall
1156 SW Westvale St
McMinnville, OR 97128-7636

From: Appellate Court Records Section Clerk

Re: Joseph Gall v. Department of Revenue
S054580
Tax Court
4767

The "Motion to waive rules for *good cause* and to review En Banc" was filed on August 11, 2009.

Response/Objection due on August 25, 2009.

COMPLIANCE WITH THE FOLLOWING IS REQUIRED:

The "Motion to waive rules for *good cause* and to review En Banc" does not conform to the Oregon Revised Statutes (ORS) and/or the Oregon Rules of Appellate Procedure (ORAP) in that:

XXX An insufficient number of copies was filed. When filing any motions, answers to motions, memorandums, and/or affidavits in the Supreme Court, one original and nine copies are required. You must submit **nine** copies. ORAP 7.10(3).

If the above-listed deficiency(ies) are not corrected within 14 days from the date of this notice, the defective document will not be considered by the court.

All documents filed with the court must include service on the opposing party(ies). ORAP 1.35(2)(a).

c: Douglas M Adair

IN THE SUPREME COURT OF THE STATE OF OREGON

August 13, 2009

To: Appellate Court Records Section Clerk

From: Joseph Gall
         1156 SW Westvale St
         McMinnville, OR 97128-7636
          Phone: 503-472-1502

Re: Joseph Gall v. Department of Revenue
          S054580
          Tax Court
          4767

The "Motion to waive rules for good cause and to review En Banc" was
filed on August 11, 2009.

In compliance with your letter of August 12, 2009 (copy attached) I am
submitting **nine** copies with this letter in person at the front window.

                              Respectfully ,
                              Joseph Gall
                              Joseph Gall, pro se Appellant

M

DEPARTMENT OF JUSTICE
GENERAL COUNSEL DIVISION

August 14, 2009

Appellate Clerk
Judicial Department
1163 State Street
Salem, OR 97301-2563

Re: *Gall v. Dept. of Revenue*
         Supreme Court Case No. S054580
         Tax Court No. 4767
         DOJ File No. 150303-GT0137-07

Dear Clerk:

Defendant, Department of Revenue, will not file a response to Plaintiff's "Motion to waive rules for *good cause* and to review En Banc" filed on August 11, 2009. Plaintiff's untimely "Motion" merely repeats or restates frivolous and groundless arguments that do not merit further response.

Sincerely,

Douglas M. Adair
Senior Assistant Attorney General
Tax & Finance Section

DMA:ckb/JUSTICE-#1570143-V1
c: Joseph Gall

IN THE SUPREME COURT OF THE STATE OF OREGON

JOSEPH GALL,
Plaintiff-Appellant,

v.

DEPARTMENT OF REVENUE,
Defendant-Respondent.

Tax Court
4767

S054580

ORDER DENYING MOTION TO WAIVE COURT RULES

Appellant's motion to waive court rules is denied.

_____
September 17, 2009
DATE

_____
CHIEF JUSTICE

c: Joseph Gall
   Douglas M Adair

gar/S054580ordy090917

ORDER DENYING MOTION TO WAIVE COURT RULES

REPLIES SHOULD BE DIRECTED TO: State Court Administrator, Records Section,
Supreme Court Building, 1163 State Street, Salem, OR 97301-2563
Page 1 of 1

Thursday, November 08, 2007

Commission on Judicial Fitness and Disability
P O Box 1130
Beaverton, OR 97075-1130

Attorney General of the State of Oregon
Office of the Solicitor General
400 Justice Building
1162 Court Street NE
Salem, OR 97301

Oregon State Bar
5200 SW Meadows Rd
Lake Oswego, OR 97035-0889

Symeon C. Symeonides
Dean and Professor of Law
Willamette University College of Law
245 Winter Street SE
Salem, OR 97301

Sheriff Crabtree
Capt Summers
Yamhill County -- State of Oregon
535 NE 5th Street
McMinnville, OR 97128

Dear Sir / Madam :

Attached to this addressee page is a five (5) page letter documenting complaints

alleging public servant incompetence and / or malfeasance.

Please be assured that everything said is truth supported by documents. If you're a
constitutional supporter -- you will most definitely become very agitated.

Joseph Gall
1156 SW Westvale St
McMinnville, OR 97128

Phone : 503-472-1502

P

Dear Sir / Madam :

What I have to say is important for the survival of our treasured constitutional Republican form of government.

First, my IQ isn't among the elite of society – I do not have a college shingle to hang on my wall; however, my country boy logic and common sense usually serves me well in the course of every day survival. Also, 76 yrs of failures and a few successes have contributed to my sense of patriotic duty to expose public corruption whenever or wherever it becomes known.

Public servants are required , in Oregon law, to be competent or be held accountable for any malfeasance in office. However, the public must rely on someone in government to prosecute. As one person, I have had no leverage to compel the District Attorney to comply with the oath he took to support the Oregon Constitution and Oregon law -- and -- the courts have failed to use their leverage to enforce the law . Unfortunately, the courts have contributed to the tyranny that grips our state through the Executive. Most average citizens lack the finances to higher a competent lawyer to go through the lengthy process and the Oregon Constitution prohibits a public servant to participate in a suit against the State. The laws are a blessing in many ways but are an abomination in other ways; however, Oregon law does demand honesty.

The purpose of this communiqué is to solicit support to expose the many recalcitrant employees in Oregon government - to seek appropriate disbarment - and to seek removal from office the judges who have aided and abetted the prevalent insurrection. Many employees of Oregon government must be held accountable.

Most egregious is the dishonest, deceitful, fraudulent misrepresentations of a case that is splashed around the world via the internet. The reader of the information does not have access to the Plaintiff-Appellant's brief (s) and motion (s) submitted nor the testimony during the trial. Our constitutional form of government provides for a redress of grievance but 'the system' has developed too many obstacles to truly achieve justice. Whenever a judge denies a motion - to my way of thinking - it is obstruction to avoid considering evidence (this happened in the course of my appeals) that doesn't fit his / her personal motives - thus, abrogating the Oregon Constitution.

Seems to me - the authors of THE CONSTITUTION OF THE UNITED STATES and THE BILL OF RIGHTS intended that a citizen should be provided an opportunity to submit a grievance , hand written on a paper sack or spoken to a government servant, and expect that it would be honestly adjudicated by a public servant; however, 'the system' has degraded the authors intentions beyond belief.

Herein, I will provide enough information to allow a competent lawyer or other public servant to read and analyze - to arrive at an independent observation of the facts.

P

My computer skills are very basic; however, the younger generation has no problem accessing the internet to research or create a web page. The addressee(s) of this communiqué should have no problem to research for facts and applicable law without blinders or personal motives.

Without doubt - money is the motivator to commit all sorts of unspeakable acts within government and / or in the public arena. In this case - it would mean losing the revenue generated from more than 65,000 mobile homes across the State of Oregon. The actual money involved could be ascertained - only if an investigator had access to government documents - the records of each county - and / or the documents at the Department of Revenue. My calculated guess is - somewhere around $26.000.000.00 (that's twenty six million dollars) or more per annum. This does not justify the illegal acts perpetrated by Oregon State public servants who threaten to confiscate our personal property if we do not pay the illegal taxation. Theft by extortion has a penalty of $250,000.00 and 10 years in prison upon conviction - this most probably is the reason that my appeals have received attack instead of honest adjudication.

The laws applicable to my personal property(my manufactured home / mobile home)have been codified for a long time. The court decision (s) have been very verbose with obfuscations intending to confuse the reader. Reference to court precedent has been used throughout - however - court precedent is not law. The law is what it is. This was stated in Plaintiff-Appellant's documents submitted. Research, by anyone, should include the entire record before splashing around the world, via the internet, the misrepresentations by the court (s) and others. Dishonesty is an abomination committed upon the entire human race.

If I had to choose only two of the TEN COMMANDMENTS they would be the eighth and ninth :

> Eighth - Thou shalt not steal ;
> Ninth - Thou shalt not bear false witness. (to lie)

Following are cases I ask you to consider :

TC 4767. SC - S 054580 Decision filed October 11, 2007 en banc by KISTLER, J.
    Plaintiff-Appellant filed a Petition for Reconsideration - response pending

Judge Breithaupt and Doug Adair must have had a pretty good round of he-hawing and back slapping when they decided the judgement for TC 4767. The conversation probably went something like this – lets show that son-of-a-bitch whos in control here – instead of fifteen hundred like before – lets make it five grand – that should shut him up – ok – go ahead Doug – you write it up and I'll sign it.

Reference to this can be found in S 054580 - the ASSIGNMENT OF ERROR !

P

OTC 4639, SC – S51473 Decision filed September 30, 2004 en banc GILLETTE, J.
Of course – the SC affirmed the lower courts judgment.

TC – MD 060207C Decision filed June 15, 2006
Plaintiff filed appeal to the Tax Court Regular Division TC 4767

Magistrate Robinson quotes ORS 307.030(1) with italics to draw attention to that part of the statute that supports the government's position - however, he overlooks "except as otherwise provided by law " ; also, he quotes ORS 308.105(1) but fails to recognize "Except as otherwise **specifically** provided ".

TC – MD 030131B Decision filed August 18, 2003
Plaintiff filed appeal to the Tax Court Regular Division TC 4639

This case was appealed as a RMV issue – because the county deceived everyone by presenting hand-outs for Measure 50 and the Department of Revenue required a Real Property appeal form. I concede ignorance but this does not exonerate those in 'the system' that should have known better. The form required to-date for manufactured homes appeal requires the use of a Real Property form (the same as before) for a petition to the Board of Property Tax Appeals (BOPTA or
BTA); however, my manufactured home/mobile home is personal property so identified by Oregon statute. This fact wasn't known by me until later – just before the case was to go to trial. It was during the trial of TC 4639 that I presented copies of ORS 308.875 - in it – it identifies my mobile home as **personal property** and it goes further to say that

'Manufactured structures classified as personal property need not be returned under ORS 308.290'. This statute was replicated in S054580 – the brief on page 12.
ORS 308.290 is the statute that establishes the requirements for filing and to declare a value for personal property .

Reasonable objectivity concludes – if a return isn't necessary then there can be no value – thus – no ad valorem tax assessment.

So – why did Judge Breithaupt rule contrary to the established facts and the applicable law ?

And – why did Justice Kistler affirm the tax court' judgment and now delays a response to my Petition for Reconsideration ?

Appellant's brief raises many, many issues ! If the court(s) do not, will not provide access to the entire record – I will – just ask.

P

Many times - the courts have advised me to consult and retain a lawyer to represent me - to get a professional opinion. You already know that I have rejected that advice but the record doesn't show the ' why ' except that I lack the finances. There are other obvious reasons as well -- such as -- a lawyer would take the case out of my hands while getting rich off my hard labor. A lawyer would not represent me, could not represent me in a suit against the government . The conflict of interest would be glaringly apparent but the lawyer would not have revealed this to me -- the client. However, it would have made it much easier to control a lawyer, to advance the governments' pervasive insurrection. The advice was dishonest, deceitful - an ethics violation..

Note that there are several individuals who have had input regards the appeals presented in Gall v Department of Revenue - individuals who have ' Adjunct Faculty' status at the Willamette University College of Law :
Judge Henry Breithaupt
Chief Judge Paul J. De Muniz
Justice W. Michael Gillette
Justice Virginia Linder

Seems to me - these folks should have recused themselves from the court deciding Gall v Department of Revenue since each of them is beneficiary of taxes collected throughout Oregon - we must include all the Supreme Court Justices - because of the conflict of interest - including Justice KISTLER, J.

I would be remiss if the following Magistrates were not included :
Magistrate Daniel K. Robinson   TC-MD 060207C
Magistrate Jeffrey S. Mattson   TC-MD 030131B

The current appeal , now with the Supreme Court - TC 4767, SC-S054580, should be reviewed by you folks with the following points to consider :

Plaintiff-Appellant did not appeal a dollar value; however the Decision
refers to Gall I and dollar value. Appellant's brief clearly states on
Page 2 paragraph 3.. in bold print - value is not the question; also
consider many other issues that a competent lawyer could easily identify as violations of law. This oversight by Justice Kistler suggests that he did not read the brief or any part of the record-- that he decided this case on a pre-conceived conspiracy.

Regardless whether or not petitioner has or has not presented the petition for redress of grievances in conformance with the Oregon Rules of Appellate Procedure - the government public servants have a responsibility to do their duty according to the law -- to consider the facts and applicable law. The rules provide for waiver in Rule 1.20. It is very doubtful that the Legislature would have approved these rules if they were too rigid. The Oregon Legislature of years past have provided for honesty in government, the pursuit of justice. Now it's time that the other two branches comply with the law.

P

Whatever I say would not be enough to truly express an adequate opinion of the experiences to-date. If you, the addressee(s), choose to live within the system as it now exists - then, I feel sorry for your children, grandchildren and beyond. The outcome of my endeavors will not affect me much either way – at 76 my days are numbered unless the good Lord has other plans.

The brief adequately states the expectations for relief from the tyrannical facilitations of the illegal tax assessment and collection.

Additionally, Willamette Law Online states "Special Assessments, when applicable by statute, are additional to the usual ad valorem process". This is quite misleading and ambiguous. Honesty demands clearly written statements that an average citizen would understand. **Special Assessments are in lieu of the usual ad valorem tax. This is evident in ORS Ch 308A .**

My hope is - that there will be appropriate disbarment, removal from office, and prosecution of all criminal conduct . The appropriate officers of this State have an obligation under statute to effect the necessary changes.

Oregon CONSTITUTION , Article VII

Section 6. Incompetency or malfeasance of public officer. Public officers shall not be impeached; but incompetency, corruption, malfeasance or delinquency in office may be tried in the same manner as criminal offenses, and judgment may be given of dismissal from office, and such further punishment as may have been prescribed by law. [Created through initiative petition filed July 7, 1910, and adopted by the people Nov. 8, 1910]

Bradley C. Berry is believed to be a current member of the Executive Committee OSB. He must recuse himself – conflict of interest – from any review of this letter . He is a subject of this complaint.

Thursday, November 08, 2007

Sincerely yours,

Joseph Gall

Joseph Gall
1156 SW Westvale St
McMinnville, OR 97128

Phone : 503-472-1502

5

P

September 22, 2009

THEODORE (TED) R. KULONGOSKI
Governor, State of Oregon
State Capitol Building
160 State Capitol
900 Court Street
Salem, Oregon 97301-4047

Cc: John R. Kroger
Attorney General of the State of Oregon
400 Justice Building
1162 Court St. N.E.
Salem, Oregon 97301-4096

REF : 1) letters to you dated; January 17, 2007 and May 17, 2007;
2) SC – S054580   TC 4767   TC-MD 060207C
3) SC – S51473   TC 4639   TC-MD 030131B

Dear Governor Kulongoski ,

Herein I will not repeat the evidence contained within the court records –
REF: 2) and 3); however, the records contain clear evidence that public
officer(s) ignored the mandates of their oath of office. Their feasance projects
itself as subjugating the law – subservient to their organized resistance to
Oregon's established constitutional Republican form of government.

Governor – this is my third appeal to you for enforcement of existing law
regards the taxation of *personal* property – manufactured homes, sited in mobile
home parks on rented space, not used as a business.

Your bio suggests a broad knowledge of Oregon and Federal law. Now, as
Governor, you have authorities and responsibilities granted or mandated in
Oregon law. It is for this reason that I now appeal to you for prosecution of the
recalcitrant public officers who knowingly and willingly colluded to perpetuate
the **illegal** taxation of *personal property*. In 1910 , the people created through
initiative petition their intentions to *criminally* prosecute these public officers –

Constitution of Oregon

ARTICLE VII (Amended)

JUDICIAL DEPARTMENT

Section 6. Incompetency or malfeasance of public officer. Public officers
shall not be impeached; but incompetency, corruption, malfeasance or
delinquency in office may be tried in the same manner as criminal offenses, and
judgment may be given of dismissal from office, and such further punishment as

1

may have been prescribed by law. [Created through initiative petition filed July 7, 1910, and adopted by the people Nov. 8, 1910]

August 11, 2009 I filed a MOTION in the Supreme Court of the State of Oregon - paragraphs 2. and 3. give just a snapshot of the entire filing –

2.

With authority of the OREGON RULES OF APPELLATE PROCEDURES – ORAP Rule 1.20 (5) – Plaintiff / Appellant petitions this court, in the interest of justice, to waive whatever rules necessary to review, to reconsider this court's decisions.

3.

RELIEF SOUGHT

Plaintiff / Appellant submits this plea to set aside the tax court DECISIONS and previous DECISIONS / ORDERS of this court.

This plea requests this court to re-instate Plaintiff / Appellant *reputation* that has been denigrated by the publishing of court decisions - court decisions that *misrepresent* established law.

Plaintiff / Appellant requests this court to award monies as stated in the BRIEF – and, refund the tax court ordered (May 11, 2009) costs and attorney fees that were not awarded by this court in its DECISION. Furthermore, Respondent did not file a timely claim in accordance with ORS 20.320.

Additionally, *sanction*, as this court sees fit in its wisdom, the recalcitrant public officers who have *knowingly and willfully* submitted false statements and claims before this court; e.g. in the RESPONDENTS' BRIEF.

However, on September 17, 2009 Chief Justice DeMuniz signed an ORDER DENYING MOTION TO WAIVE COURT RULES. This action brings into question - did someone other than the Chief Justice draft and sign the ORDER? ?without his explicit approval.

Governor, I need to know, we the people of Oregon need to know - will you direct the Oregon State Police investigate, arrest and incarcerate those named in a previous MOTION before the Supreme Court, and to include those not named - who have become complicit in Class B Felony violations? Will you support Oregon's constitutional government? Will you thwart the insurrection?

Governor, your immediate action is required to extend justice for thousands of mobile home owners of property identified in law as **personal property.** Tax statements are generally received in mid-October – statements that , in the past, contain threatening, coercive language.

A written response to this petition for redress of grievances is expected.

Sincerely,

Joseph Gall
1156 SW Westvale St
McMinnville, OR 97128

Phone: 503-472-1502

YAMHILL COUNTY
PROPERTY TAX RECEIPT   FISCAL YEAR: 2007
(503)434-7521

IN#: M00285777   AMOUNT PAID: 238.96   001 ACCOUNT#: 508939

ECEIPT NUMBER: 11535   RECEIPT DATE: 05/12/2008

AID BY: GALL JOSEPH DARLENE

EAR		LEVIED TAX	TAX PAID	FEE PAID	16% IIIT	12%IIIT/DISC	UIIPAID TAX
007	1	716.87+	238.95-			.01+	
006	1	612.35+					
005	1	498.95+					
004	1	451.67+					
003	1	575.70+					
002	1	743.54+					
001	1	920.18+					

Paid in Full

MAY 1 2 2008

Yamhill Co
Tax Collector

***** UNPAID TAX DOES NOT INCLUDE ACCRUING INTEREST *****
BALANCES AND AMOUNTS PAID IIICLUDE CORRECTIONS TO DATE

SITUS: 1156 SW WESTVALE ST
       197   MCMINNVILLE

CODES: 40.0

DONE: NO
       YES

GALL JOSEPH &
GALL DARLENE M
1156 SW WESTVALE ST
MCMINNVILLE OR 97128

Oregon

Theodore R. Kulongoski, Governor

Department of Revenue
955 Center St NE
Salem, OR 97301-2555

November 18, 2005

Mr. Joseph Gall
1156 SW Westvale Street
McMinnville, OR 97128

Re: Your letter of November 2, 2005

Dear Mr. Gall,

I have your letter of November 2 and related materials concerning your appeals in the tax court and Oregon Supreme Court. I was out of the office attending to a family matter on November 1. I will try to address your separately stated concerns as fully as I can. I encourage you to consult an attorney whom you trust if you have further questions about the way the tax laws apply to your mobile home.

First, I understand that you appealed the value assigned to your mobile home for property tax purposes for 2002-03 (Tax Court case no. 4639), 2003-04 (case no. 4675) and 2004-05 (case no. 4725). The Oregon Tax Court and the Oregon Supreme Court both considered your appeal for 2002-03, and rejected your claims. The Oregon Tax Court also dismissed your appeals for 2003-04 and 2004-05, apparently because you filed those appeals in the regular division of the Tax Court, instead of in the Magistrate Division as required by law.

In your appeal for 2002-03, you challenged the value assigned to your mobile home. It appears that you also took the position that your mobile home is not subject to property tax, but only to a $5 special assessment under ORS 308.905. Both the Tax Court and the Supreme Court rejected those arguments. They also awarded the county and the state costs and attorney fees in that case. The department of revenue then billed you for its share of the fees and costs awarded.

You were not represented by a lawyer in any of these proceedings.

You have now written to me, asserting that laws have been violated and illegal activity is taking place. I disagree.

Under Oregon law, all personal property is subject to the property tax. ORS 308.105 (1) provides: "Except as otherwise specifically provided, all personal property shall be assessed for taxation each year at its situs as of the day and hour of assessment prescribed by law."

ORS 307.190 provides: (1) All items of tangible personal property held by the owner, or for delivery by a vendor to the owner, for personal use, benefit or enjoyment, are exempt from taxation.

However, ORS 307.190(2) says: "The exemption provided in subsection (1) of this section <u>does not apply</u> to:
    (a) Any tangible personal property held by the owner, wholly or partially for use or sale in

800-075 (Rev. 1-03)

the ordinary course of a trade or business, for the production of income, or solely for investment.

(b) Any tangible personal property required to be licensed or registered under the laws of this state.

(c) Floating homes or boathouses, as defined in ORS 830.700.

(d) Manufactured structures as defined in ORS 446.561.

ORS 446.561 and ORS 446.003 define "manufactured structure" to include mobile homes and manufactured homes. In addition, ORS 820.500 (9) states, "Manufactured structures are subject to assessment and taxation under the ad valorem tax laws of this state whether or not registered under the vehicle code." ORS 801.333 defines "manufactured structure" - "'Manufactured structure' means: (a) A manufactured dwelling that is more than eight and one-half feet wide." Under these provisions of the law, it is clear that a manufactured structure, including a mobile home that is used as a personal residence, is subject to assessment and taxation under the property tax laws of this state.

There are other references in the law to taxation of manufactured structures, which include mobile homes. ORS 308.875 provides: "If the manufactured structure and the land upon which the manufactured structure is situated are owned by the same person, the assessor shall assess the manufactured structure as real property. If the manufactured structure is owned separately and apart from the land upon which it is located, it shall be assessed and taxed as personal property." ORS 308.210 states " (2) Except as provided in subsections (3) and (4) of this section, the ownership and description of all real property and manufactured structures assessed as personal property shall be shown on the assessment roll as of January 1 of such year or as it may subsequently be changed by divisions, transfers or other recorded changes." The assessor has acted lawfully under those laws.

You were entitled to ask the courts of this state to hear your position and to decide whether you were correct under the law. You did so. The courts have decided that your arguments were incorrect. As administrators of the law, neither the county assessor nor I can disregard what the courts have decided.

Property taxes are collected by the counties and distributed to cities, schools, special districts and the counties by a formula, as prescribed by law. Property taxes are then used to pay for the services provided by those government bodies.

The courts also awarded the Department of Revenue damages in the amount of $300 and attorney fees. The Tax Court awarded damages in its opinion and judgment in case no. 4639. The Supreme Court awarded attorney fees and costs in its order dated November 23, 2004, signed by the Chief Justice. That award was entered as a judgment against you on December 22, 2004. You attached both of those documents to your letter to me. You also attached a copy of a letter from Gary Humphrey to you, outlining the calculation of the costs and interest on the awards, as well as how we applied the $500 bond amount released by the Tax Court to the department.

The Department of Revenue remits those funds to the State Treasurer to be deposited in the state General Fund, which is used to pay for state services.

3

You asked me to review the "demand for payment and intent to take levy action." I agree that the language of that document appears threatening. We are required by law to inform anyone who owes the state money what remedies we have if payment isn't made. I have asked my staff to rewrite the language in a way that will satisfy the legal requirement that we provide that information, and do so in a less threatening way.

You also have asserted that Doug Adair, the Assistant Attorney General assigned to your cases, misrepresented the law. I have reviewed the materials you provided, and I have also reviewed the submissions Mr. Adair made to the Tax Court on behalf of the Department of Revenue. I believe that Mr. Adair's representations were consistent with the law. The Tax Court and Supreme Court appear to have reached the same conclusion. His role in court is to represent the interests of the State of Oregon, not the interests of an individual taxpayer.

Mr. Gall, the tax law is complex, and so are the procedures that the legislature has enacted governing appeals under those laws. As the Tax Court said in its opinion, you were advised to seek legal advice about your claims. You did not do so. You have paid the balance of the attorney fee award, and we have closed your account. You will continue to receive property tax statements each year that assess tax against your mobile home. That is appropriate, and does not violate state law.

I believe that I have answered the questions raised in your letter.

Sincerely,

Elizabeth Harchenko, Director
Oregon Department of Revenue

R

IN THE OREGON TAX COURT
Regular Division
Property Tax

1

2

3   JOSEPH GALL,   Case No. 4767

4   Plaintiff,

5   v.   GENERAL JUDGMENT

6   DEPARTMENT OF REVENUE,

7   Defendant.

8   In accordance with the court's Opinion filed November 22, 2006, and Orders filed

9   December 8, 2006, and January 24, 2007, and the conclusions set forth therein,

10   IT IS ADJUDGED that:

11   (1)   Plaintiffs' personal property manufactured home is subject to Oregon's ordinary

12   ad valorem assessment process that, in this case, properly determined a Real

13   Market and Assessed Value of $30,353 for the 2005-06 tax year;

14   (2)   Plaintiff's ad valorem tax is not limited to $6.00 by ORS 446.525;

15   (3)   Plaintiff's Assessed Value, so long as it is based on its Real Market Value, is not

16   subject to the three percent annual limitation on growth applicable to Maximum

17   Assessed Value;

18   (4)   Oregon's property tax system does not violate the Thirteenth Amendment to the

19   United States Constitution;

20   (5)   Oregon's differential assessment of recreational vehicles and manufactured homes

21   does not violate the Equal Protection Clause of the Fourteenth Amendment to the

22   United States Constitution;

23

Department of Justice
1162 Court Street NE
Salem, OR 97301-4096
(503) 947-4530 / Fax: (503) 378-6199

S

1   (6)   Plaintiff's arguments are frivolous and Defendant Department of Revenue is

2   awarded damages under ORS 305.437 in the amount of $5,000.00;

3   (7)   The Department of Revenue is denied an award of its attorney's fees under ORS

4   20.105 for failure to comply with TCR 68; and

5   (8)   The following money award is granted:

6   **MONEY AWARD FOR DEFENDANT DEPARTMENT OF REVENUE**

7   DEBTORS: Joseph Gall

8   CREDITOR: Department of Revenue, State of Oregon

9   CREDITOR'S ATTORNEY: Douglas M. Adair

10 AMOUNT: $5,000.00 in damages under ORS 305.437.

11 INTEREST: Accrues at the rate of 9% per annum, simple interest, from
                          the date the judgment is entered, until paid.

12

13   DATED this _14th_ day of _February_, 2007.

14

15

                    Henry C. Breithaupt
16   Tax Court Judge

17 Submitted by:
    Douglas M. Adair, #95195
    Assistant Attorney General
18 Oregon Department of Justice
    Of Attorneys for Defendant

19

20

21

22

23

Department of Justice
1162 Court Street NE
Salem, OR 97301-4096

USN - CPO (Ret.)
1951 - 1971

March 2009

Chief Justice Paul J. DeMuniz
Supreme Court State of Oregon

VIA

Symeon C. Symeonides
Dean and Professor of Law
Willamette University College of Law
245 Winter Street   SE
Salem, OR 97301

Your Honor :

Disclaimer first : I am merely a high school graduate; 78 yrs old; 37 yrs of government service; farm boy common sense; to stubborn to quit my appeals for justice.

Yes, I understand that you're a very busy man with not enough time to personally handle all the problems that come to your attention; and, I understand that you have delegated duties to your subordinate government employees.

Nonetheless, I do request that you consider a personal review of the facts and the law surrounding TC 4767 / S054580 as authorized in ORS 18.028.

I plead with you - consider that more than 65,000 of the poorest Oregon residents are relying on you to exercise your knowledge and authority as our advocate.

Surely you're wondering why this request is presented via Mr. Symeonides. The answer is within the attached copy of my communiqué to the Court Administrator who has not responded. Yes, I have ample reason to believe that there are subversive forces operating within the court system.

Your speeches before the Salem City Club have convinced me that you abhor anti-constitutional behavior. The ORDER of 'dismissed as moot' is not consistent with this mental picture - suggesting a subordinate made the decision without consulting you.

1

I believe the action constitutes fraud and forgery. A copy of the ORDER is attached.

Judge Breithaupt leaned on ORS 18.038 - 18.042 allowing DOR attorney Douglas M. Adair to write the judgment of the TC 4767 case. These laws defy the Oregon Constitution, Article III, Section 1. Separation of Powers.

Consequently, this lying, arrogant, bullying attorney feels free to accuse me of filing frivolous appeals - and, he repeats the accusation in his responses to my MOTION(s). Copies attached.

My appeals were not, are not frivolous but Mr. Adair had to accuse the messenger to hide his own violations of the Oregon Code of Professional Conduct.

Additionally, this attorney resented in writing when Judge Breithaupt denied his claim for attorney fees asking - para phrased - but Judge we colluded before, what has changed?.

I believe that Judge Breithaupt would like to start over - so I ask you to remand the case back to the Tax Court - to consider the court precedent set by Justice Durham in Department of Revenue v Croslin , 19 OTR 69 (2006) (S054012) , the facts and other applicable law.

I simply cannot afford to file another appeal - fearing another fine of $5,000.00; however a copy of my 2008-2009 BOPTA appeal is attached.

The illegal taxation of personal property(manufactured structure) has cost me more that $7,000.00 to fight this battle that should have been resolved during my first BOPTA hearing seven(7) years ago. The applicable law could not be more clearly stated but the misrepresentations by our public servants have resulted in a vast conspiracy to deny justice .

The current economic distress did not exist in 2002 nor did the PERS loss in the stock market. These problems should not affect a court ruling but it looks like this is exactly what happened.

Unfortunately - the Yamhill Country District Attorney , Bradley C. Berry, has refused to prosecute the assessor nor others who have aided-and-abetted the theft of these illegal taxes; however, he thinks he is qualified to fill the vacancy of deceased Judge Carol Jones. It would be a travesty if he was allowed to tarnish the bench with his sense of justice.

Some say that my writing has been too caustic and , at times , incoherent - but, this should not be a problem for college educated public servants who are mandated to be competent within their chosen profession. I offer no apologies.

We - of the mobile home community - will be most grateful if you review this case and rule in accordance with the facts and applicable law - or remand it back to the Tax Court for reconsideration.

Perhaps we are not the poorest of the poor in this State but the State's financial dilemma should not be the deciding factor.

March 19, 2009

Respectfully ,

Joseph Gall

Joseph Gall
Plaintiff-Appellant, pro se
1156 SW Westvale St
McMinnville, OR 97128-7636

Phone : 503-472-1502

November 30, 2009

Chief Justice Paul J. De Muniz
Supreme Court of the State of Oregon
1163 State Street
Salem, Oregon 97301-2563

Symeon C. Symeonides
Dean and Professor of Law
Willamette University College of Law
245 Winter Street SE
Salem, OR 97301

Ref: Gall v Dept. of Revenue : TC-MD 060207C , TC 4767 , SC-S054580
and TC-MD 030131B, TC 4639, SC S51473

Encl: 1) APPELLANT's - MOTION - Reconsider Order dtd 1-17-09
2) ORDER DENYING PETITION FOR RECONSIDERATION AND DISMISSING AS MOOT MOTION TO RECONSIDER ORDER HOLDING IN ABEYANCE dtd February 11, 2009
3) MOTION to waive rules for good cause and to review En Banc filed August 11, 2009
4) ORDER DENYING MOTION TO WAIVE COURT RULES dtd September 17, 2009

"JUSTICE DELAYED is JUSTICE DENIED"

This borrowed phrase aptly describes the reality of the criminal conspiracy to steal using the powers of government to extort payment of the illegal tax assessments affirmed by the Oregon courts.

Dear Sir:

Chief Justice DeMuniz - if you did not sign the orders of Encl : 2) and 4) - then there are clerks guilty of forgery and interference with the judicial process subject to prosecution as authorized in the Constitution of Oregon and other Oregon law. AND, the judges involved are unworthy to decide the fate of anyone.

Dean Symeonides - if you haven't - you must consider reviewing the political status of your adjunct faculty member Justice W. Michael Gillette – the Justice that affirmed the Tax Ruling in SC S51473.

Joseph Gall
Appellant, pro se

u

PROPERTY DESCRIPTION
01156 SW WESTVALE ST
MCMINNVILLE

YAMHILL COUNTY, OREGON   ACCOUNT NO: 508939
535 NE FIFTH STREET
MCMINNVILLE, OR 97128
(503) 434-7521 (HOURS: 8:30 AM-5:00 PM M-F)

PIN #: M00239797
CODE: 40.0 PCA: 0195

LAST YEAR'S TAX $451.67
See back for explanation of taxes marked with (*)

CHEMEKETA COMM COLL	18.73
MCMINNVILLE SD 40	124.15
WILLAMETTE REGIONAL ESD	8.88
EDUCATION TOTAL:	151.76

GALL JOSEPH &
GALL DARLENE M
1156 SW WESTVALE ST
MCMINNVILLE OR 97128

MH P P A	6.00
CHEMEKETA LIBRARY	2.48
MCMINNVILLE	152.37
YAM CO SOIL & WATER	1.07
YAM EMERGENCY COMM DIST	4.55
YAMHILL CO EXT SERV	1.36
YAMHILL COUNTY	78.16

VALUES:	LAST YEAR	THIS YEAR
REAL MARKET-RMV		

GENERAL GOVT TOTAL:	245.99

	LAST YEAR	THIS YEAR
STRUCTURES:	28,105	30,353
TOTAL RMV:	28,105	30,353
ASSESSED:	28,105	30,353
EXEMPTION:		

CHEMEKETA COMM COLL	10.27
MCMINNVILLE	27.31
MCMINNVILLE SD 40	63.62
BONDS - OTHER TOTAL:	101.20

NET TAXABLE:	28,105	30,353

1996 MARLETTE 27X60

TOTAL 2005-06 TAXES:	498.95

+ .9259 %

If a mortgage company pays your taxes,
This statement is for your records only.

Full Payment with 3% Discount	2/3 Payment with 2% Discount	1/3 Payment No Discount	
$483.99	$325.98	$166.32	**TOTAL TAX** (After Discount) $483.99

▲ Tear Here   PLEASE RETURN THIS PORTION WITH YOUR PAYMENT   Tear Here

2005-06 PROPERTY TAXES   YAMHILL COUNTY MFD STR   ACCOUNT NO: 508939

		Due:		
Full Payment Enclosed	......	Due:	11/15/2005	$483.99
or 2/3 Payment Enclosed	......	Due:	11/15/2005	$325.98
or 1/3 Payment Enclosed	......	Due:	11/15/2005	$166.32

DISCOUNT IS LOST & INTEREST APPLIES AFTER DUE DATE ☐ Mailing address change on back Enter Payment Amount $

MAKE PAYMENT TO:

GALL JOSEPH &
GALL DARLENE M
1156 SW WESTVALE ST
MCMINNVILLE OR 97128

YAMHILL COUNTY TAX COLLECTOR
535 N.E. 5TH
MCMINNVILLE, OR 97128

√

BEFORE THE __YAMHILL__ COUNTY BOARD OF PROPERTY TAX APPEALS

Real Property Order

In the Matter of the Petition of	)	Petition No. __#18__
Joseph Gall	)	
1156 SW Westvale Street	)	Account No. __508939__
McMinnville, Oregon 97128	)	
	)	__M00239797__

Petitioner's Name and Address

The board of property tax appeals for the County of __Yamhill__, Oregon, having duly convened on the __7th__ day of __February__, 20 __05__; and

The board, having duly considered the petition of the above-named petitioner, finds the values on the tax roll of the property described above to be sustained or reduced by the board as follows:

Real Market Value Found by Assessor:

Land	
Structures, etc.	
MS	$ 28,105
Total	$ 28,105

Real Market Value Found by Board:

Land	
Structures, etc.	
MS	$ 28,105
Total	$ 28,105

Real Market Value of Exception Found by Assessor:

Land	
Structures, etc.	
MS	
Total	

Real Market Value of Exception Found by Board:

Land	
Structures, etc.	
MS	
Total	

Maximum Assessed Value Found by Assessor:

Total	$ 55,036

Maximum Assessed Value Found by Board:

Total	$ 55,036

Assessed Value Found by Assessor:

Total	$ 28,105

Assessed Value Found by Board:

Total	$ 28,105

NOW, THEREFORE, the board hereby orders the officer in charge of the roll to sustain or reduce the tax roll of __Yamhill__ County for the tax year 2004 – 2005 in conformance with this order.

Done at __McMinnville__, Oregon this __1st__ day of __March__, 20 __05__.

By _____
Chairperson

_____
Member

_____
Member

Appeal rights — see attached.

Mailed ~~certified~~ (date) __3/16/05__ by __M Gabriel__

150-303-055-10 (Rev. 10-04)

V-1

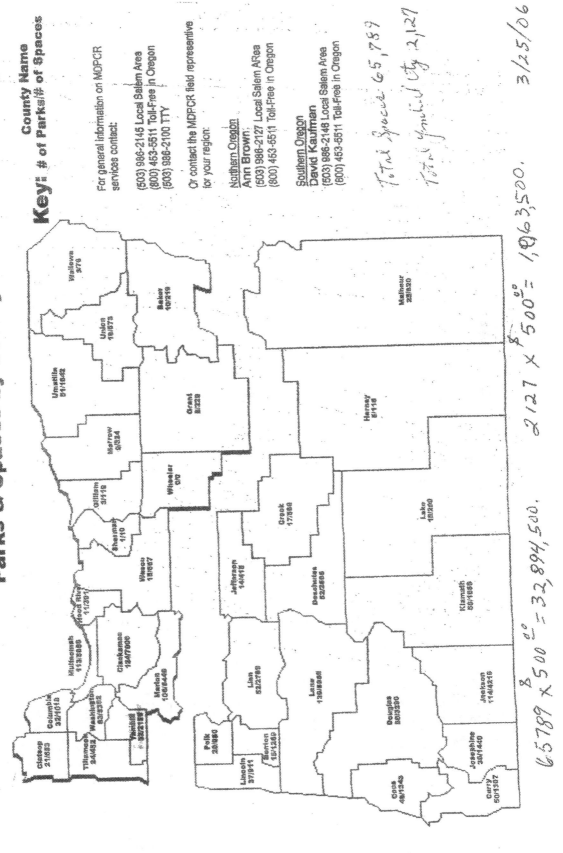

Manufactured Dwelling Park Community Relations (MDPCR)
Parks & Spaces by County

County Name
Key: # of Parks/# of Spaces

For general information on MDPCR services contact:

(503) 986-2145 Local Salem Area
(800) 453-5511 Toll-Free in Oregon
(503) 986-2100 TTY

Or contact the MDPCR field representive for your region:

Northern Oregon
Ann Brown
(503) 986-2127 Local Salem ARea
(800) 453-5511 Toll-Free in Oregon

Southern Oregon
David Kauffman
(503) 986-2145 Local Salem Area
(800) 453-5511 Toll-Free in Oregon

Total Spaces 65,789
Total Facilities 2,127

65,789 $\times$ 500.^{00} = 32,894,500.

2,127 $\times$ 500.^{00} = 1,063,500.

3/25/06

W

PROPERTY DESCRIPTION   YAMHILL COUNTY, OREGON   ACCOUNT NO: 508939
1156 SW WESTVALE ST
MCMINNVILLE   535 NE FIFTH STREET
SP 197 KATHLEEN MANOR   MCMINNVILLE, OR 97128

(503) 434-7521 (HOURS: 8:30 AM-5:00 PM M-F)

LAST YEAR'S TAX $747.92

See back for explanation of taxes marked with (*)

PIN #: M00285777
CODE: 40.0 PCA: 0195

CHEMEKETA COMM COLL	31.21
MCMINNVILLE SD 40	206.89
WILLAMETTE REGIONAL ESD	14.80
EDUCATION TOTAL:	252.90

GALL JOSEPH &
GALL DARLENE M
1156 SW WESTVALE ST
MCMINNVILLE   OR 97128

MH P P A	6.00
CHEMEKETA LIBRARY	4.14
MCMINNVILLE	253.91
YAM CO SOIL & WATER	1.79
YAMHILL CO EXT SERV	2.27
YAMHILL COUNTY	130.37
GENERAL GOVT TOTAL:	398.48

VALUES:	LAST YEAR	THIS YEAR
REAL MARKET-RMV		
STRUCTURES:	45,161	50,580
TOTAL RMV:	45,161	50,580
ASSESSED:	45,161	50,580

CHEMEKETA COMM COLL	4.18
CHEMEKETA COMM COLL ADD'L	9.18
MCMINNVILLE	41.26
MCMINNVILLE SD 40	141.39
BONDS - OTHER TOTAL:	196.01

NET TAXABLE: 45,161   50,580

TOTAL 2009-10 TAXES: 847.39

1995 MARLETTE 27X60

X.8928 %

---> PAY TAXES ONLINE AT
WWW.CO.YAMHILL.OR.US/ASSESSOR

If a mortgage company pays your taxes,
This statement is for your records only.

Full Payment with 3% Discount	2/3 Payment with 2% Discount	1/3 Payment No Discount
$821.97	$553.63	$282.47

-> NO STATEMENT SENT FOR FEBRUARY
AND/OR MAY INSTALLMENT

TOTAL TAX (After Discount) $821.97

Tear Here   Tear Here

▲ Tear Here   PLEASE RETURN THIS PORTION WITH YOUR PAYMENT   Tear Here ▲

2009-10 PROPERTY TAXES   M00285777   ACCOUNT NO: 508939

	Due:		
Full Payment Enclosed	Due:	11/16/2009	$821.97
or 2/3 Payment Enclosed	Due:	11/16/2009	$553.63
or 1/3 Payment Enclosed	Due:	11/16/2009	$282.47

DISCOUNT IS LOST & INTEREST APPLIES AFTER DUE DATE

☐ Mailing address change on back

Enter Payment Amount

$

MAKE PAYMENT TO:

GALL JOSEPH &
GALL DARLENE M
1156 SW WESTVALE ST
MCMINNVILLE   OR 97128

YAMHILL COUNTY TAX COLLECTOR
535 N.E. 5TH
MCMINNVILLE, OR 97128

150-553-008 (Rev. 6-09)

36 00508939 0000082197 0000055363 0000028247 3

Board of Property Tax Appeals
2009–2010 PERSONAL PROPERTY PETITION
and Instructions for Filing

General information

Use this form to request a reduction of the value of your taxable personal property. Personal property is taxable in Oregon if it is currently being used or being held for use in a business, or is floating property.

For the current tax year, your petition must be postmarked or delivered by December 31, 2009. See the back of this form for filing instructions.

The following information is provided to help you understand how your property is assessed.

➤ **Real Market Value (RMV)** is the value the assessor has estimated your property would sell for on the open market as of the assessment date. The assessment date for most property for the 2009–2010 tax year is January 1, 2009.

➤ **Maximum Assessed Value (MAV)** is the greater of 103 percent of the prior year's assessed value or 100 percent of the prior year's MAV. **MAV may be increased above three percent** of the prior year's assessed value if certain changes, defined as exceptions, are made to your property. Maximum assessed value does not appear on your tax statement.

➤ **Exception** means a change to property that adds value. Personal property exceptions include the addition of leased property, increased non-inventory supplies, and the acquisition of any other taxable personal property. The exception amount is derived by subtracting the prior year real market value from the current year real market value.

➤ **Assessed Value (AV)** is the value used to calculate your tax. It is the **lesser** of real market value or maximum assessed value.

Contact your county assessor for more information about how your property value was determined.

Appeal rights

Generally—Except for centrally assessed property, you may appeal the 2009–2010 real market, maximum assessed, or assessed value of your taxable personal property to the board of property tax appeals. However, the authority of BOPTA to reduce the MAV and AV of your property is **limited to the calculation allowed by law,** and an appeal may not result in a reduction of tax.

Industrial property—If you are appealing personal property that is part of a **principal or secondary industrial property** appraised by the Department of Revenue, you may file your appeal with either the Magistrate Division of the Tax Court **or** with the county board of property tax appeals. The deadline for filing your complaint with the

150-310-064 (Rev. 09-09)

Tax Court is the same as the deadline for filing with the board of property tax appeals. You may contact the Tax Court at 503-986-5650.

Centrally assessed property—The value of utilities and other centrally assessed property must be appealed to the Department of Revenue on or before June 15 of the assessment year.

Penalties—Penalties assessed for the late filing of a personal property return may also be appealed to the board of property tax appeals. Penalties should be appealed on a "Petition for Waiver of Late Filing Penalty" form.

Instructions for filing a petition

Read all instructions carefully before completing this form. If your petition is not complete, it will be returned to you. If your petition is not corrected by the date indicated on the "Defective Petition Notice" mailed to you, it will be dismissed.

Petitioner (Lines 1–10)

The owner, an owner, or any person or business that holds an interest in the property that obligates the person or business to pay the property taxes is legally authorized to appeal to the board of property tax appeals. If the person or business is not the owner or does not receive the tax statement, **proof of an obligation to pay the taxes must be submitted with the petition.** Contracts and lease agreements are examples of documents that may allow a party other than the owner to appeal.

If property is owned by a business, the petition (or authorization to represent, if applicable) must be signed by a person who can legally bind the company. For most corporations, this is usually a corporate officer. **Employees regularly employed in tax matters for a corporation or other business may also sign the petition.**

If you need help in determining who can sign the petition for your business or other organization, contact the county clerk's office in your county.

Authorized representative (Lines 11–22)

The law allows only certain people to sign the petition and appear at the hearing to represent the petitioner.

Those people who need a signed authorization from the petitioner in order to sign the petition include:

- A relative of the owner(s). Relative is defined as: spouse, (step)son, (step)daughter, (step)brother, (step)sister, (step)father, (step)mother, grandchild, grandparent, nephew, niece, son- or daughter-in-law, brother- or sister-in-law, father- or mother-in-law.

Board of Property Tax Appeals
2009–2010 PERSONAL PROPERTY PETITION

for   YAMHILL   County

- Read all instructions carefully before completing this form.
- Please print or type the requested information on both sides of this petition.
- Complete one petition form for each account you are appealing.
- Return your completed petition(s) to the address shown on the back.
- Please attach a copy of your tax statement.
- If you wish to appeal the value of a manufactured structure, use the Real Property Petition (150-310-063) instead of this petition.

Petitioner (Person in whose name petition is filed)

1 Check the box that applies: [X] Owner
    [ ] Person or business, other than owner, obligated to pay taxes (attach proof of obligation)

2 Name—individual, corporation, or other business	3 Telephone number		
Joseph Gall	Daytime (503) 472-1502	Evening ( )	

4 Mailing address (street or PO Box)	5 City	6 State	7 ZIP code	8 E-mail address (optional)
1156 SW Westvale St	McMinnville	OR	97128	

FOR BUSINESS USE ONLY

9 Name of person acting for corporation, LLC, or other business	10 Title (i.e., president, vice president, tax manager, etc.)
Not applicable	

If a representative is named on line 11, all correspondence regarding this petition will be mailed or delivered to the representative.

Representative } To be completed when petition is signed by an authorized representative of petitioner. Only certain people qualify to act as an authorized representative. See the instructions for a list of who qualifies.

11 Name of representative	12 Telephone number		
Not applicable	Daytime ( )	Evening ( )	

13 Mailing address (street or PO Box)	14 City	15 State	16 ZIP code	17 E-mail address (optional)
N/A				

18 Relationship to petitioner named on line 2
N/A

19 Oregon state bar number	20 Oregon appraiser license number	21 Oregon broker license number	22 Oregon CPA or PA permit or S.E.A. number
N/A			

Any refund resulting from this appeal will be made payable to the petitioner named on line 2 unless separate written authorization is made to the county tax collector.

Attendance at Hearing :   YES , I wish to attend

23 [ ]   Check this box if you do not wish to be present or be represented at the hearing. If you choose to not be present at the hearing, the board will make a decision based on the written evidence you submit.

Property Information

24 Assessor's account number (from your tax statement)	25 Code area number (from your tax statement)
508939	CODE: 40.0 PCA: 0195 PIN #:M00285777

26 Street address and city where property is located	27 Property type [ ] Retail [ ] Industrial [ ] Floating Property [ ] Office
1156 SW Westvale St	[ ] Motel/Apartment [ ] Small Manufacturing [ ] Food Service [X] Other

Y-1

Attach additional pages if necessary.

Description of item, category, or schedule	Real Market Value (RMV) from assessor's records	RMV Requested
28 Manufactured Structure	$ 50,580.00	$ "0"
29	$	$
30	$	$
31	$	$
32 Total RMV →	$ 50,580.00	$ "0"

	Assessed Value (AV) from tax statement or assessor's records	AV is limited to the calculation allowed by law
33 Total Assessed Value (AV) →	$ 50,580.00	

Evidence of Property Value Attach documentation such as recent purchase agreements, bills of sale, appraisals (attach complete report), or other information.

34 Why do you think the value of your property is incorrect? (Answer the question in the space provided or by attaching additional pages. Provide enough information to support the value(s) you are requesting. Be specific.)

This manufactured structure is PERSONAL property(ORS 308.875);personal property is tax exempt(ORS 307.190); value reporting is waived(ORS 308.875,ORS 308.290)thus establishing a "0"tax base; the LEGISLATURE created a SPECIAL assessment of $6.for a specific purpose (ORS 446.525);BOPTA is required to take an "oath" to support ALL laws(Constitution of Oregon, Article XV, Section 3.)(ORS 309.070); BOPTA is required to be competent(ORS 162.4 this tax constitutes theft and extortion(ORS164.075);Secondarily, the assessed value(AV) of nearly 9% violates the limitation imposed by law(ORS 308.149, ORS 307.032)

35 Did you purchase the property within the past three years? ☐ Yes ☒ No If yes, complete the following:

Date purchased: _____ Purchase Price: _____

Did you purchase the property at an auction? ☐ Yes ☒ No If yes, where? _____

36 Have you sold or attempted to sell the property within the past three years? ☐ Yes ☒ No If yes, complete the following:

Sales / Asking price: _____ Date sold or dates offered for sale: _____

37 Has your property been appraised within the past three years? ☐ Yes ☒ No If yes, complete the following:

Appraised value: _____ Date of appraisal: _____

Purpose of appraisal: _____ Name of appraiser: _____

Declaration: I declare under the penalties for false swearing [ORS 305.990(4)] that I have examined this document, and to the best of my knowledge, it is true, correct, and complete.

38 Signature and name of petitioner or petitioner's representative (attach authorization if necessary)		39 Date
X _Joseph Gall_ Sign name	Joseph Gall Print or type name	_Nov 8 2009_

When and where to file your petition

Appeal petitions must be filed with the board of property tax appeals by **December 31, 2009.** File your petition with the county clerk in the county where the property is located. Do not file your petition with the county assessor. Mail or deliver your petition to the address shown in the box. →

Please return this petition to:

Y-2

November 08, 2009

FROM :   Joseph Gall , 1156 SW Westvale St
         McMinnville, OR 97128-7636
TO :   Board of Property Tax Appeals(BOPTA)
         Yamhill County, Oregon
SUBJ :   2009-2010 PERSONAL PROPERTY PETITION
         Form 150-310-064(Rev. 09-09) signed Nov 8, 2009

This is a continuation , addendum , to the statements on line 34.

306.220 Compliance of public officers with laws and orders affecting property taxes.
(1) Every public officer shall comply with any lawful order, rule or regulation of the Department of Revenue made under ORS 306.115, 308.335 or 309.400.

(2) Whenever it appears to the department that any public officer or employee whose duties relate to the assessment or equalization of assessments of property for taxation has failed to comply with any law relating to such duties, or the rules of the department made in pursuance thereof, the department, after an informal conference on the facts, may direct the public officer or employee to comply with such law or rule.

(3) If the public officer or employee, for a period of 10 days after service on the public officer or employee of the department's direction, neglects or refuses to comply therewith, the department may apply to the Oregon Tax Court for an order, returnable within five days from the date thereof, to compel the public officer or employee to comply with the law or rule, or to show cause why the public officer or employee should not be compelled so to do.

(4) Any order issued by the judge pursuant thereto shall be final.

(5) The remedy provided in this section shall be cumulative and shall not preclude the department from exercising any power or rights delegated to it. [Amended by 1983 c.605 §4; 1993 c.18 §67; 1995 c.650 §69; 1999 c.21 §13]

Petitioner's Note : ORS 306.115, 308.335, 309.400 heaps all the responsibility on the back of the assessors; and, the statement on the cover page of 150-310-064(Rev.09-09) (first paragraph) states "Personal property is taxable in Oregon if it is currently being used or being held for use in a business, or is floating property". BOPTA BEWARE you'll also be thrown to the wolves ! (CYA) when the Constitution is enforced.

Page one of one

Y-3